"A student of Scripture and se[...]
us that sexuality is a divine gi[...] [...]ingly how
that is so and why it matters. God created sexuality for his glory and our
good, and we must think his thoughts after him about it."

David B. Garner, Dean of Faculty and Vice President of Global Ministries,
Westminster Theological Seminary

"We need discipleship in the area of sexuality, which is more than a clearer
version of the 'birds and bees' talk our parents may (or may not) have given
us. We need to learn to think biblically and talk conversationally about sexuality. That is what David White provides in *God, You, & Sex*."

Brad Hambrick, Pastor of Counseling, The Summit Church, Durham,
NC; general editor for *Becoming a Church that Cares Well for the Abused*
(churchcares.com)

"*God, You, & Sex* is a book for everyone. It is timely, honest, readable, and
vulnerably practical. Walk with David White through the joys and pleasures,
pain and shame, as well as the brokenness and delight of sexuality in a fallen
world. You will discover God's grace and hope all along the way."

Peter A. Lillback, President, Westminster Theological Seminary, Philadelphia

"David White articulates God's story on sex with faithfulness and clarity,
offering us the perspective we need to both live and teach about sex in all its
glory *to* God's glory!"

Walt Mueller, The Center for Parent/Youth Understanding

"Sometimes one reads a book and finds it radically different than what one
expected. I just didn't expect the game-changing nature of this book. I don't
believe I'll think about God's gift of our sexuality the same way ever again.
Read it and rejoice . . . and thank me for commending it to you."

Steve Brown, Broadcaster; seminary professor; author of *Talk the Walk*

"*God, You, & Sex* invites the believer to think biblically about their sexuality.
Its pages paint a bigger and bolder perspective on how the Life-giver calls us
to be life-givers both biologically and spiritually. This resource is foundational
for singles and married alike."

Karen Hodge, Coordinator for Women's Ministries, Presbyterian Church
in America; author of *Transformed: Life-taker to Life-giver* and *Life-
giving Leadership*

"In the presently over-served Christian market of books on sex, this is the
'one more book on sex' that *needed* to be written. David White shows an
unusually deep understanding of the spiritual meaning of God-created human
sexuality, so needed in our day of frenzied sexual obsession."

Peter Jones, Director, *truthXchange*; adjunct professor, Westminster
Seminary California; author of *The God of Sex*

"To the one who wondered if sex was better than chocolate, David White's
God, You, & Sex says a resounding yes. But White proves that sex is also a
fearful mystery—of God's passionate love for the Bride. Let those who would
enjoy its pleasures hold to God's sure terms of use."

Andrée Seu Peterson, Senior writer, *World* magazine

"David White raises the stakes as he leads us to consider how created and redeemed sexuality leads us deeper into our relationship with God. I warmly commend his work."

Liam Goligher, Senior Minister, Tenth Presbyterian Church, Philadelphia

"In the midst of widespread cultural confusion and sexual brokenness, this book is an excellent tool for any Christ follower seeking to develop and nurture a healthy view of sexuality."

Hunter Beless, Host, *Journeywomen* podcast

"With a tender pastoral heart, David weaves compassion through his biblical treatment of sex, marriage, and singleness, aware that he is speaking into a broken world. This is a book every Christian should read and that pastors and counselors should plan to keep on supply to give away."

Marty Machowski, Family pastor; author of *God Made Boys and Girls, The Ology, Long Story Short*, and other gospel-rich resources

"With great wisdom and the tender care of a pastor, White teaches that sex and sexuality are ultimately about God and our relationship with him in Christ. David has written a timely word and a book that deserves a wide reading."

Raymond Johnson, Senior Pastor of Christ Church West Chester, West Chester, PA; author of *I See Dead People: The Function of the Resurrection of the Saints in Matthew 27:51–54*

"All too often people view sexuality quite narrowly on a horizontal level, but David White rightly challenges his readers to include the vertical perspective—to include God, the creator of sex—and what a difference it makes! This book will help you personally, it will help your marriage, it will help your church, and it will help you interact with others on these challenging subjects."

Timothy Witmer, Emeritus Professor of Practical Theology, Westminster Theological Seminary, Philadelphia; author of *The Shepherd Leader*

"David gives us the needed message that not just sex, but other features of relationships like falling in love are 'very good.' His decades of experience mean that his advice is never trite, is sensitive to the variety of experiences with sex that people have, and encompasses contemporary problems."

Sam A. Andreades, Pastor; speaker; author of *enGendered* and the blog, *Affirming Gender*

"You'll learn a lot from White's direct and gracious handling of all the thorny, contemporary issues of sex and sexual expression, but most of all you'll see how God's heart longs for you and how yours can respond to him in return."

William P. Smith, Senior Pastor for Renewal Main Line; author of *Parenting with Words of Grace* and numerous other books and booklets

God, You, & Sex

A Profound Mystery

DAVID WHITE

New
Growth
Press
WWW.NEWGROWTHPRESS.COM

New Growth Press, Greensboro, NC 27404
www.newgrowthpress.com

Cover Design: Faceout Books, faceoutstudio.com
Interior Typesetting and eBook: lparnellbookservices.com

ISBN: 978-1-948130-75-2 (Print)
ISBN: 978-1-948130-84-4 (eBook)

Library of Congress Cataloging-in-Publication Data
Names: White, David, 1970– author.
Title: God, you, & sex : a profound mystery / David White.
Other titles: God, you, and sex
Description: Greensboro, NC : New Growth Press, 2019. | Includes bib-
    liographical references.
Identifiers: LCCN 2019022084 (print) | ISBN 9781948130752 (pbk.)
Subjects: LCSH: Sex—Religious aspects—Christianity.
Classification: LCC BT708 .W4285 2019 (print) | LCC BT708 (ebook) |
    DDC 233/.5—dc23
LC record available at https://lccn.loc.gov/2019022084
LC ebook record available at https://lccn.loc.gov/2019981562

Printed in the United States of America

26 25 24 23 22 21 20 19   2 3 4 5 6

Contents

For Jennifer,
bone of my bone and flesh of my flesh

"Therefore a man shall leave his father and mother
and hold fast to his wife,
and the two shall become one flesh."
This mystery is profound, and I am saying
that it refers to Christ and the church.

Ephesians 5:31–32

Foreword

There is a catalog of adjectives you could use to describe a good book,

thoughtful

provocative

thorough

insightful

practical

illuminating

biblical

approachable,

and I would use all of these terms to describe this wonderful book. But there is another term that immediately came to mind as I worked my way through what White has gifted us with in this book, *timely*. It would be hard to imagine a book that could speak with more helpfulness and clarity to this cultural moment than the book you're now reading. It would not be an overstatement to say that sex is everywhere around us and yet almost nowhere understood. In some way, sex hits you every day—from its use in advertising, its constant presence in entertainment, its use as a political tool, and its dominance on the internet—it's virtually impossible to avoid. In case you haven't noticed, you live in a culture that is so sex-focused it is nearly sex-obsessed. It has so infiltrated the oxygen of our culture that it is almost impossible not to breathe it in. Sadly, little of the sex talk that is in the air around is good, true, honorable, wholesome, or faithful to the Creator's design.

So, we need writers who will take on this topic, not in a way that is overly critical, defensive, protective, or in some way sex-negative. But rather in a way that celebrates this beautiful gift from the Creator's hand and then helps us to understand what it has been designed to be—not just so we can escape harm, but so we can celebrate it in a way that submits to and worships the Giver more than the gift. Having read this book, I am convinced that David White is just the type of writer I have described. Let me explain to you why I think this is so.

1. *He understands the individual, corporate, cultural, and church confusion about sex.* From advertising to erotica, sex has been misrepresented, misused, misunderstood, and poorly defined. As you read, you will realize that White doesn't just understand this confusion from the helicopter view as a theoretician, but also at street level. He has walked through that confusion himself; he has given many years of his life and ministry to walk through that confusion with others, leading them to a greater understanding and the personal freedom of biblical clarity. He knows well the confusing siren voice of temptation, the confusing pain of past misuse and abuse, and the confusing hurt of regret. He is able to speak into the confusion with a simplicity of wisdom that is so needed in the middle of the din of so many conflicting voices.

2. *He understands that you simply cannot understand sex horizontally.* Sex comes from God, so it connects you to God whether you know it or not, and because it does, it is always an act of the worship of something. Perhaps the most powerful part of this book is its discussion of how sex reveals God to us and is meant to connect us to the kind of relationship to him that grace makes possible. White powerfully demonstrates to us

that it is only when you understand sex vertically that you will experience in horizontal human relationship what it was designed to be, experiencing and celebrating its beauty.

3. *He understands that sex connects you to the deepest and scariest of questions.* There are two cries in the heart of every human being. The first is, "Will someone love me?" The second is even scarier, "Once they get to know me, will they still love me?" These questions are answered first and foremost by the self-sacrificing love of the Lord Jesus. He was willing to die so that we would know the joy and security of active, eternal, unshakable love, the kind of love you could never earn and that won't be taken away when you mess up. White knows that one of the things that makes sex sacred and holy is that the self-sacrificing, patient, tender, vulnerable, other-centeredness of sex between a man and a woman in marriage is meant to be a visible representation of God's love for us in Christ Jesus.

4. *He understands that sex, like any other form of pleasure, requires boundaries.* White understands that God created pleasure, and to enjoy the pleasures he created brings him glory. But he also understands that pleasure without boundaries never goes anywhere good. God's boundaries are not put in place to rob us of pleasure, but so that we can be fully free to enjoy those pleasures in a way that does not harm us or harm our intimacy with him and others. White knows that pleasure isn't ultimate—God is; and remembering this, is where safe sex begins.

5. *Finally, he understands that the Bible is not sex-negative.* I would imagine that if you asked people on the street about the Bible and sex, the bulk of them would communicate that the Bible leaves little room for us to be free to enjoy sexual pleasure. But David White

knows that the Bible celebrates a God who is good and who blesses us with good things. Sex, as designed by God and enjoyed inside of God's boundaries, is a very good and beautiful gift from the hand of a wise and loving Creator. So, the Bible does not understand sex as a bad and dangerous thing, but rather understands that any good thing God gives us becomes a bad thing when it is used, enjoyed, or manipulated outside of God's loving and protective plan.

So, White has penned here a very needed and timely book. It is a welcomed note of sanity and clarity in a moment of massive insanity and confusion when it comes to sex. It will clarify your thinking while it makes you thankful for God's good gift and the wisdom he gives us as to how that gift is to be used.

Paul David Tripp
7/14/19

Introduction

Do we really need another Christian book about sex? We have plenty of books decrying pornography and homosexuality, numerous how-to manuals expositing the Song of Solomon for married couples, and many books explaining and defending the Bible's teaching on sexuality. Such books are often helpful and commendable. However, I have been concerned by the relative absence of a central feature of the Bible's teaching on sexuality . . .

Sex is about God. He invites us into a deeper understanding of who he is by creating us in his image as sexual beings. Because this is a fundamental aspect of our humanity, regardless of whether we are single or married, all Christians have much to learn about God through their sexuality. God is a God of pleasure, intending that all his good gifts would lead us to a deeper relationship with him. So, this audacious claim that sex is about God flows from the reality that God is our Creator who delights to infuse creation with experiences of pleasure. Humanity is distinct from the rest of the created order because we are fashioned in the image of God. As God's image-bearers, our sexual differentiation as male and female and, for some of us, our sexual practice in heterosexual marriage are ways God reveals himself to the world—calling out to all creation, "I AM!" The goal of this book is to develop a positive, biblical theology of sex grounded in this conviction.

Sex is about God and you. As the gospel story unfolds, Scripture depicts an ever-increasing intimacy with our Creator God, culminating with Jesus revealed as the ultimate Bridegroom. God created marriage as the context for sexuality so that we would have an understanding of his relationship with us! One of the most remarkable statements in the Bible about sexuality comes from Paul's letter to the Ephesians. While teaching about marriage, Paul referred to God's intention at creation, concluding with an amazing statement, "'Therefore a man shall leave his father and mother and hold fast to his wife, and the two shall become one flesh.' This mystery is profound, and I am saying that it refers to Christ and the church" (Ephesians 5:31–32). As with the discovery of a new island or deeper oceanic trench, this mystery has wonders that need to be explored! What does it mean that marriage is about Jesus and the church? How does Jesus as our Bridegroom impact our understanding of what it means to be his? What can we learn about our relationship with God through our romantic drive and our longings to love and be loved? How does the intensity of sexual desire reveal something God wants us to know about his heart toward us?

The New Testament teaches that the love of God is the foundation for our entire lives: "God is love, and whoever abides in love abides in God" (1 John 4:16). In the Old Testament, God rescued Israel from slavery—a great act of love—that led to the greatest commandment for life with him: "You shall love the LORD your God with all your heart and with all your soul and with all your might" (Deuteronomy 6:5; also see Matthew 22:37–38). A mutual exchange of love is fundamental to who we are: "We love because he first loved us" (1 John 4:19). We are commanded to love God yet told that our love is reciprocal, flowing from his initiation. Reciprocal love, given and received in the context of God-ordained relationships, is central to what it means to be human and to the gospel of Jesus. As we will see, a biblical understanding of sexual love is anchored in this redemptive reality. Since falling in love is one of the most glorious human experiences, it is incredibly important to see God's love for us in this glorious light. We are created with a romantic drive because God's heart has the passion of a lover! When we fail to see Jesus as our Bridegroom or even our Lover, we are short-circuiting our understanding of his love and, therefore, the potential depths of our love for God. What this means is that *the gospel* is at the heart of human sexuality. Our reluctance to broadly proclaim God's design for sexuality is actually a hindrance to the proclamation of the gospel to a lost and dying world that's obsessed with sex but blind to its true glory.

Sex is good. Much has been distorted by a fallen world, and our own hearts are pulled in many unholy sexual directions. But sexuality remains part of God's good creation. After making humanity male and female in his image—the crowning achievement of all creation—God looked over his vast handiwork and declared it "very good" (Genesis 1:31). Though sexuality often becomes twisted in opposition to God's design, it still remains good. Neither the sexual decadence of our culture nor our shame over our own broken sexuality should prevent us from loudly declaring God as the creator of this good gift and giving him glory as the Giver.

Unless we understand sexuality is ultimately about God and our relationship with him, we will not have a complete picture of the God we worship. Christians have a wonderful opportunity to help people inside and outside the church learn that sex is glorious because its Creator is infinitely more so. The delight we experience through romance, pursuit, and passion are dramas intended to point beyond themselves to the One who came to pursue his beloved, even though this love meant passing through trials, suffering, and death. Every good fairy tale or story of heroism reflects the greatest love story, the wonder of the love of God for us, which is shown in the Son who came to rescue his bride held by the darkest enemy in the deepest pit, so that we might all *really* live happily ever after. But understanding the passion and heart of the Rescuer is too often absent from our meditation and proclamation of the gospel. I love how C. S. Lewis describes the infinite bliss awaiting us, foreshadowed in the gift of sexuality: "The happiness which God designs for His higher creatures is the happiness of being freely, voluntarily united to Him and to each other in an ecstasy of love and delight compared with which the most rapturous love between a man and a woman on this earth is mere milk and water."[1] There is glory in our current experience of sexuality, but it is a dim shadow of the wonders awaiting us.

Why These Things Matter

Sex is in our face more than ever before. The sexual revolution has finally come to bitter fruition as teens and young adults increasingly shun relationships, embracing the hookup culture. The rise of the internet and the more recent proliferation of mobile devices has made pornography cheaper, more accessible, and easier to hide. The cultural message is clear: sex brings life. Denying the tug of your flesh relegates you to a shrunken existence. In the face of these messages and the pervasiveness of sexual temptation, Christian men and women need a compelling reason to obey God with their sexuality.

For almost twenty years I have served at Harvest USA, a Christian ministry helping men and women overcome sexual sin. (There's a real need for all those books that have been written!) I have also been educating churches in America from coast to coast about these issues. In this work I have observed several concerning trends.

First, pornography use is growing in the church and there seems to be an increasing acceptance that this is "just the way things are." This is exacerbated by an approach to Christianity that values personal authenticity more than holiness and is wary of any teaching that sounds legalistic. In our current situation we urgently need to recover the gospel truth that our sexuality is about God and our relationship to him. This needs to be the foundation for any teaching on sexual behavior.

Second, while the world is obsessed with sex, the church remains either silent or confused in its teachings about sex. Although sexuality is a good gift from God, too often the church's message has been limited to making sure all the prohibitions are crystal clear and instructing teens to wait for marriage. On the other extreme, some Christians embrace sexuality with a zeal that seems to baptize the world's obsession by focusing on enhancing pleasure without considering God's design for sexual practice in marriage. The church needs to have a balanced, biblical approach to proclaiming the goodness of sexuality as it points to God and his relationship with us.

Third, a significant culture shift has occurred among Christians in recent generations regarding sexuality. My experience with Christians under thirty-five is that many are unashamedly sexually active in their serious relationships. There is growing confusion about what the Bible means when it refers to sexual immorality. Many millennial Christians think only intercourse really counts. Some Christian writers suggest traditional morality is too uptight and there should be some permissible sexual activities prior to marriage, commensurate with the seriousness of the relationship. Not only does this add to the current confusion, it encourages sinful behavior that wounds individuals when relationships fail, and it erodes the fullness of delight that God wants them to experience should they enter marriage.

Fourth, there has been a recent seismic shift in evangelical views on same-sex intimacy. Now that the *Obergefell v. Hodges* decision has made gay marriage the law of the land, there is greater acceptance in the church. Prominent Christians in the media and increasing numbers of younger evangelicals are giving enthusiastic support to same-sex relationships. But most pastors do not seem to realize this shift has been underway for a long time. The average Christian spends far more time consuming secular media and entertainment than in prayer, Scripture, or fellowship with other believers. Further, many younger Christians believe homosexuality should be placed within the narrative of God's good creation, rather than a consequence of the fall into sin. Unlike a generation ago, most Christians personally know someone who experiences same-sex attraction, and these personal connections help shape those Christians' convictions about sexuality. While we need compassion for those who have suffered bullying, exclusion, and other mistreatment, Christian sexual ethics need to be rooted in Scripture. Only there do we learn how our sexuality points beyond itself to our mysterious union with God.

Who This Book Is For

My prayer is that this book will enable you to see God's romantic heart for you. It is beautiful and secure to be loved by a parent. There is joy and excitement in a sibling relationship. Friendship provides comfort, affirmation, and intimacy. But despite all the blessings of these human relationships, which reflect our relationship with God, to be delighted in and desired by the Lover is life-changing. My hope is that, as you spend time in prayer, read the Bible, and sit quietly in God's presence, this book will help your sexuality become an avenue in which you are able to worship God in deeper ways because you have an increasing awareness of his love and desire for intimacy with you.

Having greater awareness that sexuality points to God and his relationship with you will inevitably help you in the challenges you face sexually. I am convinced that one tactic of the enemy is to cause us to separate these two things. He's ruthlessly committed to keeping you from learning the depths of God's love for you, and he seeks to thwart our love and worship at every turn. Growing to see God as your Lover provides a new approach to resisting the world, the flesh, and the devil.

The church also faces increasing antagonism from the wider culture. I suspect you have had the experience of mentioning to an unbeliever that you are a Christian and then being asked, "So, do you hate gays?" I want Christians to have a thorough biblical understanding of why God's design for sex is a lifelong union between a man and a woman. And I want you to be able to connect Christian sexual ethics to a broader Christian worldview.

Likewise, I want to offer guidance to Christian parents on how to help their children develop a healthy sexuality. More than simply telling our kids, "Wait until you're married," this book will equip you to connect your children's sexuality to the rest of their life in Christ, and, in age-appropriate ways, help your kids see God in a wonderful, new light. This is incredibly important as they approach the teen years and begin to wrestle with their emerging sexual desires. We'll consider many of the issues confronting your kids and provide talking points for navigating those conversations. No parent relishes these talks, but it is critical for parenting in the twenty-first century.

This May Be Hard for You . . .

These pages will be easiest to read for those who are happily married and who experience a passionate and fulfilling sex life. Your experience of this good gift naturally leads to worship of the Giver. But that's a small percentage of people who will pick up this book. So my prayer is the chapters that follow will be more helpful to people who are *not* in that category.

All marriages involve pain and challenges, and it is possible that, as you read this book, you are in a very difficult marriage. Your experience of this relationship, and maybe sex specifically, has been fraught with deep pain and disappointment.

While all couples struggle with sex in some fashion, many also struggle with an inability to conceive children. Whatever your particular struggles, the following pages may seem to be a mockery of your trial. I hope you will see that Jesus profoundly understands the brokenness of life and marriage in a fallen world. He is not removed from suffering. The "man of sorrows" (Isaiah 53:3) was wounded by his beloved repeatedly in countless ways. He understands your experience and wants to meet you in your pain. He also perseveres in love, so he knows the grace you need so you will "not be overcome by evil, but overcome evil with good" (Romans 12:21).

If you are single, I am most eager for you to read this and be encouraged by God's heart for you. The experience of singleness can be incredibly difficult. I am poignantly aware of the limitations of a book in assuaging the sadness of lost or unfulfilled hopes. "Hope deferred makes the heart sick" (Proverbs 13:12). But I pray that the One who understands the challenge of singleness through his own human experience will meet you in these pages and assure you that there is an "eternal weight of glory" coming that renders all our current struggles light and momentary by comparison (2 Corinthians 4:17–18).

If you are unmarried and struggle with same-sex attraction, you face additional challenges. Perhaps you believe heterosexual marriage is impossible for you. My hope is that as you read this book, the issue of your sexuality will be gathered up into God's incredible work of redemption, so as your identity is more firmly rooted in him, you will find an ability to rest in Jesus, the ultimate Bridegroom.

If you are a survivor of sexual abuse, any discussion of sexuality can be jarring. If you have not processed your traumatic past with a counselor, I would encourage you to consider this as an important part of healing. Even if you have, reading this may still be hard. When your experience of something beautiful has been defiled, it can be deeply troubling to be repeatedly told that it really *is* glorious. With that disclaimer, this book is about how sex points us to Jesus. Although sexuality is profoundly broken in this world, the hope of the gospel is the renewal of all things. The end of the gospel story is re-creation, when the entire cosmos will be made new, every tear will be wiped away, and every pain will be healed. In the great words of J. R. R. Tolkien, the day is coming when everything sad will come untrue.[2] I hope in these pages your eyes will be lifted beyond your suffering in this world to glimpse the glory awaiting you and the avenging and undoing of all your suffering. One day the world will be made right.

Sexual Redemption: My Story

You may be curious why someone would spend nearly twenty years working in a ministry specifically devoted to helping sexually broken people, as well as teaching the church about sex, sexuality, and gender. I am a man who experienced profound brokenness in my sexuality but wondrous redemption. I was exposed to pornography as a young child. There are some things you can never forget, like when your friend who lives next door says, "You'll never believe what I found in the basement . . ." This led to a lot of confusion because as a preschooler, I did not know how to process this information. Not to mention the feelings of guilt and shame. Despite my confusion, I intuitively knew looking at these images was wrong. Childhood sexual play with another neighbor compounded my confusion, guilt, and shame. Everything was further exacerbated as I hit puberty, discovered masturbation, began stealing porn magazines from the local drugstore, and watched hard-core films on VHS tapes with friends. Eventually I became sexually active and brought a porn worldview into my real-world experience.

Two decades after my first sexual exposure, I came to faith at twenty-four. The Spirit of God worked in dramatic ways.

Incredibly, my insatiable desire for porn dissipated.[3] I praise God for delivering me from this struggle before the internet was a standard household utility, mercifully sparing me from the scourge of online porn. Equally astounding (for a single guy in my twenties), I found incredible freedom from masturbation. So by God's amazing grace, I didn't bring overt, technicolor sexual sin into my marriage, but the undoing of all that past sin, as well as the worldview behind it, took a long time. It was years before there was appropriate freedom and joy in my sexual experience. Therefore, I write as one who has experienced *redemption* in this area of life. By God's grace, I now experience a sexuality that leads to worship of God and a deepening emotional and spiritual oneness with my wife.

There is a further twist to my story of intimacy and sexuality. I had been teaching that sex was about Jesus for almost a decade when my first wife, Sandy, passed away suddenly from a blood infection following her first chemo treatment for breast cancer. As I continued to teach these things, I had a profound awareness that God wanted me to *live* them. During that season of singleness, I needed to experience the hope of Jesus as my "spouse" in the face of unsatisfied desires. God used this experience to impress this deeply on my heart and to prepare me for my current marriage to Jennifer.

I am not saying that I have it all together. I battle temptation daily, and I need to continually ask for grace to love Jennifer well and holistically. But I write with *hope*. I have experienced the goodness of God as he's brought freedom to an area of my life where I once was enslaved. I want to share aspects of this transformation as a means of encouragement, realizing that many readers wrestle intensely with their sexuality. Not everyone has sunk to my depths (though others have gone deeper), but we all have a sexuality impacted by sin. All of us need sexual redemption so that we, with pure hearts, may have eyes to see God through the lens of our sexuality and that it—even in abstinence—might lead us to him. I pray the following reflections will be transformative, leading you deeper into the profound mystery of Jesus's love.

It Is Always Just a Signpost

One of the dangers in writing a positive Christian book on sexuality is that sexuality can be made to assume an inordinately important place in the Christian life. Since there has been so much silence in the church, it is easy to have the pendulum swing too far in the opposite direction. Some pastors started encouraging married couples to have sex every day. Others have suggested means to make sex more pleasurable or exciting. These are examples of well-intended leaders overcompensating for past silence and missing the importance of the fact that our sexuality is meant to lead us to *God*. Accordingly, what we must keep central is the way our various experiences of sex, chastity, and even sorrow lead us to Jesus, the ultimate Bridegroom. Sex has been a source of great idolatry since the first fall into sin. But if we understand it rightly, it will lead us to worship.

We need to always keep in mind that sex, even at its best, is only a signpost. It points to the Giver of life but will never be the source of lasting contentment, happiness, or life. It should lead to right worship but never become an object of worship. There are seeds of idolatry buried in any experience of pleasure because we are so prone to supplant the Giver with the gift. Sexual experience will always be more like a piece of chocolate cake than a source of life. It is a gift to be received with thanksgiving that should lead to a heart of increasing gratitude, but it will not change your life. Only living in relationship with the Lover of your soul will do that. But the delight of this signpost should thrill us to anticipate what it will mean to see Jesus face to face.

CHAPTER 1

Sex and God

There has been a lot of bad press in recent years about Christianity and sex. The prevailing notion in secular culture seems to be that Christianity is repressive and negative about sex. Where did this idea come from? You will not find it in the Bible! Scripture unashamedly teaches that sex is a good gift from God that he invites us to delight in. God rejoices in human sexuality. Most people are only aware of the ways the Bible limits sexual activity. Admittedly, these restraints seem to go against the grain of our natural tendencies. But the guardrails God places around sexuality aren't just for our practical good, they are absolutely critical to understanding the "profound mystery" that sex points to God's love and delight in us.

Tragically, the church has done little to help the cultural conversation. The typical approach to sexuality has been embarrassed silence. Of course, there are notable exceptions. It's not hard to find fiery sermons against adultery and homosexuality, many of which ignore the real-life sexual struggles of Christians in the congregation. And then there is the youth pastor, whose job description usually includes an annual, "Wait until you're married!" Sunday school lesson. The fact that the Bible's restrictions on sexuality are often counter to our sexual inclinations, as well as our failure to communicate the wonder and beauty of God's design, are significant reasons why millennials are leaving the American church in droves.[1]

Apart from a clear articulation of how sexuality reflects the gospel, the mandates of lifelong, heterosexual marriage seem arbitrary and antiquated. Further, I work with many millennials who grew up in the church and received only negative messages about sexuality, which caused significant challenges once they entered marriage. Ill-equipped to joyfully embrace their God-given sexuality, they experience shame and guilt in the very area of married life that should deepen intimacy and oneness.

Prudish or shame-based views of sexuality are foreign to the Bible. From Genesis to Revelation, the Bible is unashamedly positive about marital sexuality. As we will see, a robust understanding of God's design for human sexuality is a beautiful proclamation of the gospel promise that God will be our God and we will be his people.

Seeing and Hearing "I AM"

All of life is about God. From all of creation his voice calls to us, wooing those who have eyes to see and ears to hear. This reality is echoed beautifully in these lines from Elizabeth Barrett Browning's epic poem, "Aurora Leigh":

> Earth's crammed with heaven,
> And every common bush afire with God;
> But only he who sees, takes off his shoes—
> The rest sit round and pluck blackberries.[2]

When God appeared to Moses in the burning bush, instructing him to remove his shoes, he revealed his name to be YHWH, meaning "I AM," expressing his self-existence (see Exodus 3:13–15). In all areas of life, God cries out, "I AM!" Psalm 19:1 announces, "The heavens declare the glory of God, and the sky above proclaims his handiwork." But God's glory is not seen only through brilliant, billowing clouds or a sunset over the Grand Canyon. He is calling out to us through every facet of existence. The delights of sex invite us to approach the God of sex. Yet most of us do not take off our shoes to worship; instead we pursue earthly pleasures, oblivious to the Giver of gifts.

Sexuality Reflects Our Relational Creator

As Scripture unfolds, we read how marriage and sexuality are infused with glory, but the very first chapter of the Bible hints at this profound mystery. The first hint of the Christian teaching that God is a Trinity—three persons in one being—is found in the creation story, in which God, who has existed in relationship for all eternity, creates not a singular being but a couple to mirror his image to the world. The first chapter of the Bible teaches that humanity is modeled after the "community life" of our Creator, and marriage in particular serves to express this characteristic.

> Then God said, "Let us make man in our image, after our likeness. And let them have dominion over the fish of the sea and over the birds of the heavens and over the livestock and over all the earth and over every creeping thing that creeps on the earth."
> So God created man in his own image,
>   in the image of God he created him;
>   male and female he created them.
> And God blessed them. And God said to them, "Be fruitful and multiply and fill the earth and subdue it, and have dominion over the fish of the sea and over the birds of the heavens and over every living thing that moves on the earth." (Genesis 1:26–28)

By indicating that the first humans were made "in the image of God," the Bible sets them apart from the rest of the created order. Of all the creatures in the world, this designation is for humanity alone. And, importantly, this image includes sexual *diversity* as part of its expression. Though sexual differentiation is something that humanity shares with the rest of the animal world, nevertheless the created plurality of the human family appears to reflect the nature of the God whose image we bear. Did you notice the interplay of nouns and pronouns that refer to God in the passage? In verse 26, God (singular) says "Let *us* make man in *our* image" (plural). In verse 27, humanity was made in "*his* own image" (singular). The same pronoun dance occurs as verse 27 continues to describe humanity: "He created *him*" (singular) followed by "he created *them*" (plural). Why is there this shifting between the singular and plural? It appears that God is one and yet is also able to speak of himself in communal terms; likewise, humanity is singular, yet differentiated into diverse members of a nevertheless unified family. This is the first hint of the glorious unity and diversity within the Trinity and within the human community the triune God created.

We only get glimpses of the triune, communal nature of God in the Old Testament, but as redemptive history moves to the fullness of God's revelation in Jesus, the New Testament teaches that God exists as Father, Son, and Holy Spirit. This is especially evident in texts such as the baptism of Jesus in Matthew 3:16–17, where all three persons are present.[3] The Trinity means that all three persons of God existed together in personal relationship from eternity past. The creation of two sexes reflects God's existence as a communal being. God's complementary existence as Father, Son, and Spirit—most gloriously displayed through their corporate work for the redemption of humanity—is depicted in the complementary relationships in human sexuality. Like a child's shoebox diorama of the Rocky Mountains, human sexuality is a tiny picture of the divine reality that shaped the cosmos.

This means *love predated creation*. Because of God's trinitarian existence, when the Bible teaches "God is love" (1 John 4:8, 16), we understand this is literally true! God's personhood has always existed in an eternal relationship of love. As C. S. Lewis wrote, "[Christians] believe that the living, dynamic activity of love has been going on in God forever and has created everything else."[4] The created universe is the overflow of God's trinitarian love. Because God *is* love, he created a universe to have even more to love. And he designed a diverse humanity as his image-bearers to reflect the wonder of his love.

Corresponding Puzzle Pieces

After Genesis 1 provides the broad brushstrokes, Genesis 2 zooms in to look at the formation of humanity. God first creates Adam, making a single being from the dust of the ground, and places him "in the garden of Eden to work and keep it" (Genesis 2:15). Then we read something astonishing. After the repeated refrain throughout Genesis 1, in which we hear that "God saw that it was good," the Creator now looks at his handiwork and makes a jarring assessment, "It is *not good* that the man should be alone; I will make him a helper fit for him" (v. 18, emphasis added). His specific concern is humanity's solitary existence—Adam is alone and needs a helper fit for him. The Hebrew is important here because a more literal translation would be "a helper like opposite him."[5] Adam does not need a duplicate but an individual who mirrors him and corresponds to him, like puzzle pieces fitted together. And since both sexual intimacy and procreation are clearly part of this design (see Genesis 1:28; 2:24–25), this complementarity of male and female is distinctly sexual. There are obvious implications for this when we consider God's design for marriage. God's intention at creation was *complementary* partners, uniquely crafted to be fitted to one other. Although this applies to physical, sexual differentiation, as we'll see, this

"fittedness" transcends our physicality. The unique complementarity of male and female is further expressed through the
emotional and spiritual oneness fostered in marriage.

But how did this creation of two different, related humans
happen? Prior to resolving the problem of humanity's solitary existence, God dramatizes that problem, drawing it into
focus. He creates the animal kingdom and parades it before
Adam, who names each of the animals as they appear. "But
for Adam there was not found a helper fit for him" (Genesis 2:20). The absence of a partner, which God had declared
to be "not good," was thus made part of the man's *experience*. I think it's a safe bet that Adam felt something was off.
We may imagine his mounting unease: with each successive
incompatible partner, his gnawing sense of aloneness grew.
Would there *ever* be someone with whom he *fits*? Apparently
even in paradise God wanted his children to trust him and to
wait for his provision.

And so, in God's time, "the LORD God caused a deep sleep
to fall upon the man, and while he slept took one of his ribs
and closed up its place with flesh" (Genesis 2:21). This is the
only time this Hebrew word is applied to the human body.
Elsewhere, it refers to the rings "on the side" of the ark or a
man walking along a "hillside." As we consider what follows, I
think it's helpful to see this surgery as a "splitting asunder" of
Adam, rather than the simple removal of a bone. (As an aside, I
remember being told as a child that men have one rib less than
women. Let me set the record straight here: ribs are always
paired, and most men and women have twelve pairs.) God
seems to work against his original creation of Adam, taking
apart what he had previously made in order to make something new, something better. It creates a situation in which
humanity is no longer complete without relational union. Just
as the woman's existence comes about because of the man, so
man's existence in his present form is fundamentally shaped by
the creation of the woman and his relation to her. Adam does

not remain unchanged in the process of Eve's creation; both man and woman are what they are because of one another.

It is against this background of two humans formed from one another that we hear the archetypal love poem: "Then the man said, 'This *at last* is bone of my bones and flesh of my flesh; she shall be called Woman, because she was taken out of Man.' Therefore a man shall leave his father and his mother and hold fast to his wife, and they shall become one flesh" (Genesis 2:23–24, emphasis added).

After facing life without a helper, the man is now over-joyed. The period of waiting for the Lord to act has been worth it. Although we are not privy to how he knows the informa-tion, Adam is clearly aware Eve was taken out of him and that therefore they belong together.

So, what is at the heart of the marriage union? The single image of God separated into the two sexes is reunited in a physical union powerful enough to create *life*. This is why John Stott commented that while it is possible for humans to have various sorts of sexual relations, only in marriage does a *reunion* occur. Reflecting on Genesis 2, Stott wrote, "It is the union of two persons who originally were one, were then separated from each other, and now in the sexual encounter of marriage come together again."[6] And it is because God has reunited what was once separated that Jesus commands us to honor marriage: "What therefore God has joined together, let not man put asunder" (Mark 10:9, RSV).

Stop for a moment and think about this. In married sexu-ality, the image-bearers of God, who were torn asunder, are brought back together in profound pleasure that generates life. In the pleasurable experience of sexual union, we reflect the joy of union within the Trinity. Married love is thus a reflec-tion—imperfect but real—of the glorious existence of the Father, Son, and Spirit as they've lived in perfect harmony, joy, and pleasure together from eternity past.[7] With sex as in all of life, God is calling out to us "I AM!" and inviting us to worship him. In this way, wedded sexuality is profoundly God-like. It should lead married couples to deeper worship.

Babies Matter

I mentioned at the beginning of this chapter that we are sexual beings because we are creatures. This is how God designed us to produce offspring, and it is something we share with the rest of the created order. But, despite the creatureliness of our procreation, this too points us to the wonder of our Creator. It is easy to see the power of sexual addiction rooted in pleasure. But this pleasure is inextricably linked in God's design to the ability to produce life. This is a significant reflection of the *power* of sex that ultimately comes from God, who alone is the Giver of life.[8]

Can you feel the creative exuberance in Genesis 1 as God commands everything he has made to flourish, reproduce, and fill the earth? Beginning with plant life, which is endowed with seed for reproduction (v. 11), God commands all his creatures to "be fruitful and multiply" (v. 22, sea creatures and birds; v. 24, animals on dry land; v. 28, humanity). While the production of offspring is not the only purpose of sex—as we have seen, sex is about *God*—nevertheless, procreation is a central function of God's design for sexuality. Although sex is for *more* than procreation, and although not all married couples are able to have children, it is important to highlight this aspect of human sexuality because sex is widely viewed as primarily a recreational activity today. But as we think about biblical sexuality, it is crucial to acknowledge that *one aspect* of God's creational intention for sex is that it would produce fruit.

As the author of life, God designed sexual activity to include the potential of creating life. God desires that all of his creation would reflect back his beauty and fruitfulness. Biblical sexuality does not mean married couples should care only about procreation, and it does not diminish the beauty of sexuality for couples unable to conceive. But we should always have in mind that this physical act was intended to bring forth life.

Sexuality as the means of producing offspring points to a God of abundant life. God's design of sexual differentiation, especially since humanity is made in his image, provides a reflection of the delight experienced within the eternal three-in-one relationship within the Trinity. Keep in mind though, we are always seeing only tiny glimpses—little snatches of light, fleeting moments of clarity—as we try to understand mysteries infinitely beyond our creaturely capabilities. Our loving God provides these signposts to spur us on in our pursuit of him.

It's about Oneness

The true invitation of image-bearing sexuality is to be naked and not ashamed. This is the last glorious snapshot of pre-fall humanity: "And the man and his wife were both naked and were not ashamed" (Genesis 2:25). To be made in the image of God means we are created for relationship (with God and others) and *intimacy*. God's intention for marriage is a relationship in which we are known and accepted. This is one of the reasons the enemy hates marital sexuality so much—it reflects our Creator as his power and goodness are on display in the realm of human relations.

While writing this book I officiated the wedding ceremony for two of my good friends. They asked me to include in their service this quote from Tim Keller, which articulates the power of married love: "To be loved but not known is comforting but superficial. To be known and not loved is our greatest fear. But to be fully known and truly loved is, well, a lot like being loved by God. It is what we need more than anything. It liberates us from pretense, humbles us out of our self-righteousness, and fortifies us for any difficulty life can throw at us."[9]

This loss of our original unashamed nakedness helps to explain why feelings of loneliness can be exacerbated when we are surrounded by other people. It is so painful to *not* be known by others, yet the way of the world causes us to live in isolation from one another. One of the loneliest seasons of my life was when I was a college student living in a little efficiency apartment in downtown Philadelphia. In the midst of a near-constant crowd, I was deeply hurting but no one knew or had the capacity to help. Being surrounded by people all the time while feeling "unknown" made everything worse.

We long to be truly known by others, but at the same time we are incredibly fearful of being exposed. All of us live with some sense of shame, believing that if others *really* knew us, they'd reject us. So, we're trapped in a classic Catch-22. We long to be known, and, simultaneously, we deeply fear intimacy. This primal fear of exposure lives in our human relationships, but it is fundamentally rooted in our estrangement from God. Prior to the fall into sin, marriage was the original context in which people were "naked and unashamed" in the sight of one another and were walking together in fellowship with God. The devastation of sin ruptured this picture entirely—our intimacy with one another has been stolen, but so has our intimacy with God. Through his self-sacrificing love, Jesus restores us to himself and to one another. In Christ, we are free from shame and free to be known. This freedom comes from being naked and unashamed before the only One whose love and appraisal of us truly matters. Because of Jesus, we are assured of acceptance. Even though he knew all the worst things about us, he "came to seek and to save the lost" (Luke 19:10). It is an astounding reality that "God shows his love for us in that while we were still sinners, Christ died for us" (Romans 5:8). First Corinthians 13:12 points forward to the day when we will know fully, even as we are fully known by him now.

This deep, profound knowing—free from shame—is the destiny of redeemed humanity. We are invited to taste that now in our present relationships as we grow in intimacy with one another. When I am living in the hope of God's reconciling love toward me in Christ, I am free for those closest to me to know the worst things about me. In fact, I embrace transparency because I realize how much I need the rest of the body of Christ to reach maturity (see Ephesians 4:15–16). God intends for this intimacy to be at the heart of every marriage—a willingness to be absolutely naked and vulnerable with another human being in every way. This deepest human intimacy, rooted in emotional and spiritual oneness, is what separates human sexuality from the mere mating of our fellow creatures.

There is a reason why the word used frequently in the Hebrew Bible to describe sexual activity is *yada*, which means "to know." This reflects the wonder of image-bearing sexuality. This naked and unashamed *knowing* is the culminating celebration of the emotional and spiritual union created by marriage. Marital sexual union is so much more than physical coupling because humanity has emotional and spiritual depth unlike other creatures. We are created to be truly known in a one-flesh relationship because we are image-bearers. It is the coming together emotionally and spiritually, as well as physically, that makes human sexuality a reflection of our Creator.

I entered marriage to my late wife as a new believer with a sinful past, so there was a long road ahead of undoing the attitudes and approaches I'd developed around sex. Formerly, I approached romantic relationships with a view toward my sexual experience. But after being married for several months, I had a profound experience that marked the beginning of a shift in my perspective on sex and its place in my marriage. At the end of a long day, we were getting ready for bed and having a great conversation. As we sat on the bed together in various stages of undress, the thought flitted through my brain, *I wonder if we're going to have sex after this?* My next thought was a completely novel work of the Spirit: *Actually, it really doesn't matter because this conversation is amazing!* More than twenty years later, I can't remember what we were talking about. And, beautifully, I can't remember if we had sex afterwards. What stuck with me was the realization that I was connecting with my wife emotionally and spiritually in a way that I had never experienced before, in a way that was thrilling and actually transcended physical intimacy. Sexual pleasure had *always* mattered more to me. But on that evening I discovered something deeper. And this deeper "one-flesh" reality of marital intimacy points to the most wondrous, profound mystery of all: our relationship to God through our union with Jesus.

CHAPTER 2

God as Our Lover

As incredible as it sounds that sexuality gives a glimpse into relationship within the Godhead, there is more: God created marriage and sexuality for us to know his heart toward us! Beginning with the Old Testament prophets, God's relationship to his people was described as a faithful husband to his faithless bride. Some of these passages are astonishing. Consider one of the earliest, Jeremiah 2:1–2: "The word of the LORD came to me, saying, 'Go and proclaim in the hearing of Jerusalem, Thus says the LORD, "I remember the devotion of your youth, your love as a bride, how you followed me in the wilderness, in a land not sown." '"

This statement is shocking for anyone who's read the book of Numbers! The journey through the wilderness recounts one incident after another of Israel grumbling against the Lord. Worry, complain, grumble. God delivers. Repeat. I once heard an NPR commentator describe the history of Israel, "They were in the land of Egypt, and they kvetched. God brought them to the Red Sea, and they kvetched. He brought them to Mount Sinai, and they kvetched . . ." (*Kvetch* means to complain habitually.)[1] Pause for a moment and revel in God's selective memory! His recollection of Israel's wilderness wandering is surprisingly different than the record of the historical books. I praise God that my "life is hidden with Christ in

God" (Colossians 3:3) and that the Father sees me in Christ and looks at my life with the same selective memory.

But the standard use of the marriage metaphor in the Old Testament is to demonstrate Israel's faithlessness to God. Marital infidelity is used to illustrate the horror of idolatry. God tells his people that the closest human experience that approximates what idolatry does to his heart is adultery. If you have suffered this terrible betrayal, you know something of the travail of our Savior's heart. This is the dark side of the creation of marriage as an institution. In a fallen world, the call to total fidelity opens the door to betrayal and deep pain. Many of the Old Testament passages contain stirring declarations of God's love and devotion, followed by the people's rejection. One of the most frequent descriptions of Israel's idolatry is "whoring" after other gods. Because (tragically) many of us know the profound pain of a violated covenant, sexual betrayal is used in the Bible to demonstrate the anguish of idolatry to the heart of our ultimate Bridegroom.

Shortly after Jeremiah recounts the "memory" of Israel's faithfulness, God laments the current state of affairs:

> For long ago I broke your yoke
>   and burst your bonds;
>   but you said, "I will not serve."
> Yes, on every high hill
>   and under every green tree
>   you bowed down like a whore.
> Yet I planted you a choice vine,
>   wholly of pure seed.
> How then have you turned degenerate
>   and become a wild vine?
> Though you wash yourself with lye
>   and use much soap,
>   the stain of your guilt is still before me,
> declares the LORD GOD.

How can you say, "I am not unclean,
    I have not gone after the Baals"?
Look at your way in the valley;
    know what you have done—
a restless young camel running here and there,
    a wild donkey used to the wilderness,
in her heat sniffing the wind!
    Who can restrain her lust?
None who seek her need weary themselves;
    in her month they will find her.
Keep your feet from going unshod
    and your throat from thirst.
But you said, "It is hopeless,
    for I have loved foreigners,
    and after them I will go." (Jeremiah 2:20–25)

Can you sense God's distress in this passage, his heart-ache over his people's illicit trysts? He longs for closeness, intimacy, and devotion. He is a jealous God desiring an exclusive relationship. But his people prefer running around with other lovers.

The book of Ezekiel contains two stirring accounts where God's relationship with his people is described in terms of sexual love in a marital covenant. Ezekiel 16, in particular, communicates God's dedication and delight in his people. He found Israel as a forsaken infant, cast out and despised. He rescued her from dying of exposure and enabled her to flourish. The passage describes her body maturing as she reached "the age for love" (v. 8), then God claimed her for his own, making a vow and entering into a covenant. With tender care he washed her and anointed her with oil. He lavishly clothed her as a princess in fine linen and silk, adorning her with gold and silver bracelets, necklace, earrings, and crown. God clothed and adorned his beloved bride extravagantly and fed her royally.

But this deep devotion and loving attention to all her needs is repaid with scorn. Israel bitterly betrays God as she flirts with other lovers. Unlike a prostitute, who is at least compensated for her immorality, Israel gives away her riches to her paramours. All the gifts lavished on her by God are wantonly distributed among her lovers from the other nations. God accuses Israel of "offering yourself to any passerby and multiplying your whoring" (v. 25). And this is a euphemistic rendering. The Hebrew graphically recounts "you spread your legs to any passerby." God loved his bride and lavished riches upon her, enabling her to be esteemed by all the surrounding nations, but in her folly she debases herself.

The same metaphor of adultery is used in Ezekiel 23 when God portrays Samaria and Jerusalem as two whoring sisters.[2] The cities are rebuked for abandoning God's protection and care to run after the nations of Egypt, Assyria, and Babylon. They sought alliances with them and worshiped their gods. Stark and shocking images of adultery are employed. The sisters are described as burning with lust toward the military officers, longing for their breasts to be fondled (vv. 3, 8, 21). After Samaria's destruction, instead of learning from her demise, Jerusalem intensifies her adultery with Babylon. She lusts after the men described as having "members" like donkeys and "issue" like horses (v. 20). God presents these shocking images as a broken-hearted husband. He has been made a cuckold and an object of mocking derision.

These pictures remind me of my experience as an unbelieving undergraduate. I had a friend whose beautiful girlfriend (a student at another college) was notoriously promiscuous. Her roommate dated another of my friends, so everyone but her boyfriend knew what was going on. It was awful. This poor, doting guy was being played for a fool. That is the picture provided in these passages of God's relationship with his people. Adultery is a tragically tangible expression of the terrible pain of idolatry to God's heart.

In both passages, there is a sense of God's compounding anguish as the depth of Israel's betrayal increases. All the wealth and care bestowed on her is given to her lovers. Even the precious children born to her are slaughtered before her lovers (the idols of the nations). Yet, despite his heartache over her unfaithfulness, God promises to remain faithful. In the face of her wanton promiscuity, God declares, "Yet I will remember my covenant with you in the days of your youth, and I will establish for you an everlasting covenant" (Ezekiel 16:60). Further, in a wondrous expectation of what he will accomplish in Christ, he promises to "atone for you for all that you have done" (v. 63). In the face of judgment in the Old Testament, this promise is a glimmer of hope foreshadowing the coming of Christ and the gospel. Ezekiel 36 and 37 build toward the promise of "circumcised hearts" and the outpouring of God's Spirit, which will result in the dead being resurrected, and ultimately culminates with one of my favorite pictures of "new creation" in all of Scripture in Ezekiel 47:1–12.

The marriage metaphor is deepened in Hosea 1–3, when God calls the prophet Hosea to painfully dramatize Israel's spiritual state.[3] Hosea's own marriage becomes a living parable before the people of their spiritual adultery. "When the LORD first spoke through Hosea, the LORD said to Hosea, 'Go, take to yourself a wife of whoredom and have children of whoredom, for the land commits great whoredom by forsaking the LORD' " (Hosea 1:2). God calls Hosea to painfully portray the underbelly of the marriage metaphor in his own life. This set the stage for judgment against Israel but also demonstrated God's faithfulness and ultimate redemption. After Hosea took Gomer to be his wife, she "conceived and bore him a son" (v. 3), and he was named Jezreel, meaning "God will sow." But then she conceives two more children, who were not attributed to Hosea—a daughter named No Mercy and a son named Not My People (vv. 6, 9). The absence of the clear pronouncement of Hosea's paternity suggests that these are the "children of whoredom" God commanded Hosea to embrace as his own.[4] And, of course, the names of these children foretold judgment—God removed his mercy and forsook the northern kingdom of Israel as his people.

But amid the declarations of judgment, God continues to proclaim his amazing grace. The judgment against Israel is ultimately for her good. After pouring out his blessing on her, God vows to strip away everything, leaving Israel naked and ravaged. But the great hope in Hosea is that God remains utterly committed to his initial promises. He declares, "Therefore I will hedge up her way with thorns, and I will build a wall against her, so that she cannot find her paths" (Hosea 2:6).

Did you catch the reason for his discipline? He thwarts her pursuit of other lovers and reins in her paths so that she will find her way back to him! "She shall pursue her lovers but not overtake them, and she shall seek them but shall not find them. Then she shall say, 'I will go and return to my first husband, for it was better for me then than now'" (v. 7). God's discipline is specifically focused on the renewal of the relationship with his beloved.

The point in all of this is that God, who is full of love toward his wayward people, looks for a responding love. Hosea anticipates the sweetness of Israel's repentance and reconciled relationship: "'In that day,' declares the LORD, 'you will call me "my husband"; you will no longer call me "my master"'" (2:16 NIV).

God boldly proclaims his goal in this relationship: oneness—union with his beloved. He wants to take us deeper than merely the relationship of a creature before its Creator. He wants us to know the fullness of what it means that we are created in his image. So he declares through Hosea: "And I will betroth you to me forever. I will betroth you to me in righteousness and in justice, in steadfast love and in mercy. I will betroth you to me in faithfulness. And you shall know the LORD" (2:19–20). In a beautiful anticipation of Jesus's pursuit of his bride when he pays the price for our redemption with his own blood, Hosea "buys back" his wife, redeeming her and embracing Gomer as his own (see Hosea 3). And God's severe judgment is overturned as he declares, "And I will have mercy on No Mercy, and I will say to Not My People, 'You are my people'; and he shall say, 'You are my God'" (Hosea 2:23).

Therefore, despite the warnings and judgment, despite the reality that the marriage metaphor was significantly employed to use the motif of adultery to underscore Israel's sin against their faithful God, the final word (as always!) is God's goodness and commitment to *his promises to his people*.

A Lover's Delight

One of the incredible implications of the marriage metaphor is that God has a lover's delight for his people. Most of us have set categories for thinking about God. Certainly through Christ's work in his death and resurrection, we know him as the Savior and Redeemer. For those who are well steeped in the Psalms, perhaps you gravitate to descriptions like our refuge, rock, shield, or strong tower. For lots of very good reasons (the Lord's Prayer chief among them), we've become comfortable talking about God as our Father. And there are other familial relationships in view. We refer to Jesus as our elder brother, perhaps even friend. We've grown very accustomed with these portrayals, but one of the most profound and wondrous is often neglected: Jesus as our Lover and Bridegroom. Although the prophets usually riff on the marriage metaphor in the negative sense (depicting idolatry as adultery), there are some astoundingly beautiful pictures of God as the lover with his beloved, delighting in his people.

After cataloguing the sins of Judah and warning of impending judgment, Zephaniah concludes with a glorious passage filled with joy and amazing declarations of God's love for his people. Beginning with the invitation, "Sing aloud,

O daughter of Zion; shout, O Israel! Rejoice and exult with all your heart, O daughter of Jerusalem!" (Zephaniah 3:14), the passage describes that God would remove his judgment and sweep away all Israel's enemies. They "shall never again fear evil" (3:15). Although Zephaniah never explicitly mentions the marriage metaphor, consider this amazing description of God's love for his people, "The LORD your God is in your midst, a mighty one who will save; he will rejoice over you with gladness; he will quiet you by his love; he will exult over you with loud singing" (Zephaniah 3:17). I suspect that this is a familiar verse to many readers, so we need to pause and consider afresh these incredible descriptions.

"*The* LORD *your God is in your midst.*" You are not alone. As we go through life's trials, experiencing pain, crushing disappointment, and agonizing heartache, we're tempted to believe we've been abandoned. But just like Hagar, pregnant and languishing in the wilderness, we are invited to learn "You are the God who sees me" (Genesis 16:13 NIV). And with the outpouring of the Spirit, this is infinitely greater than even Zephaniah imagined. The indwelling of the Spirit means that God is not just around us and attentive to our lives (as amazing as this was in the Old Testament), but the Spirit is actually *inside* us, experiencing all the ups and downs of your life. He is riding the rollercoaster with you, experiencing what you experience and feeling what you feel. This is part of the reason that "the Spirit himself intercedes for us with groanings too deep for words" (Romans 8:26). As you walk through the challenges and travails of life in a fallen world, God is in you, experiencing these things, too, with the closeness of a lover.

"*A mighty one who will save.*" I know, at least sometimes, you are keenly aware of your finitude. You experience it in all your relationships when the "going gets tough." There are times you know you're not tough enough to "get going." You experience it in your work life in the face of hopeless deadlines or unattainable expectations. These are actually the sanest moments in your life. As a dear friend frequently says, "Life is not hard—it's impossible!" After all, you are just a puny creature in this vast world. You weren't designed to face life alone. You were created to be *consciously carried* through this life by the One who's promised to be your Deliverer and is powerful beyond your comprehension. (Open your favorite Bible app and revisit some of the astounding descriptions in Isaiah 40 right now if you need a refresher. God spans the universe with his fingers and holds the Pacific Ocean in the palm of his hand!) Know that he carries you like a little lamb whether you realize it or not. We need "saving," not only in an eternal, freedom-from-sin sense, but also every day of our lives. And he is faithful.

"He will rejoice over you with gladness." It's the look of sheer joy on your dear friend's face as you open the perfect birthday gift she knew you'd love. A child's dashing, almost-knock-you-down embrace around your knees after a business trip. The contented sigh you hear as you hug that special grandparent you get to see only once a year. What's in view with this statement is the rejoicing that comes purely from *relationship*. No externals and frills, just the utter delight in *you* as a human being. God created you, exactly as you are, and he rejoices over you. His gladness trembles with delight, expectation, and longing.

"He will quiet you by his love." You know what it's like to console someone who's in distress. After a child's terror-stricken nightmare, you say gentle, soothing words as you gather him up onto your lap with a tender embrace. Or you hold the anguished, heartbroken friend, encouraging her that she's not alone and won't be rejected by you or others in your circle of friends. The suffocating anxiety and heart-racing panic gives way as you embrace, pray, and point to the One who is in control. Or perhaps it's you who are consoled. After suffering an injustice and experiencing surging rage, you're calmed as a brother grips your shoulders, reminding you of the One who

said, "Peace! Be still!" (Mark 4:39) and promises to avenge. Finite creatures are easily agitated. Anxiety, frustration, and sadness are never far away in a fallen world. We need tender words spoken and the palpable comfort of *presence*. These are human snapshots of the promised Comforter, given to lead us into truth, quiet our fears, assure us of the promises fulfilled, fuel our hope, and give us undiminished joy. Closer to our main topic, a powerful human picture is a spouse who knows you deeply, understands your pain, embraces you tenderly, and knows the right words to speak to your aching heart. This is a fitting image of God's love for us—our ultimate Bridegroom embraces and soothes, assuring us of his love and good plan for our lives.

"*He will exult over you with loud singing.*" Any one of the previous statements standing alone would be incredible. They are life-giving portraits of God in relationship to us. But this last one is mind-boggling. Pause and take this in: *God's rejoicing over you is so intense only raucous singing suffices.* This is not a gentle, lover's serenade. Romeo beneath Juliet's window doesn't come close. Zephaniah's portrayal holds together the tenderness of lovers with the roar of a sports crowd. It's Romeo crossed with Philadelphia Eagles fans at the victory parade, singing "Fly, Eagles, fly!" How many things in life fill you with such joy that you want to sing? I realize this may be more characteristic for theater-types than engineers, but what brings about exuberant emotion that floods out of you unhindered? For God, it's his people—even you, as an individual. Do you believe this?

A couple days ago I walked into our family room to find one of our daughters rewatching *The Empire Strikes Back*. It was the climactic scene where Yoda raises the X-wing fighter out of the swamp, followed by Luke's breathless reply, "I don't believe it." If I am honest, that's often my response to these biblical truths. Maybe this is you right now. Ask God for eyes to see and a heart softened to these truths. The One who rejoices in you and sings over you, wants you to know the truth of his passion for you. He does not want these to be abstract theological propositions, but life-giving promises that fuel deepening conversations with him, bolster your trust in life's storms, and enable you to love others selflessly and hold loosely to the things of this world as you place your hope in the world to come. Like all lovers, God wants a response of delighted love, joy, and exuberance. He wants us to know the tender intimacy of a lover.

A Lover in the Darkness

I mentioned earlier my first wife's passing. That grief was ago-nizing on so many levels as I faced the loss of a woman I deeply loved. After she died, it was as if all the challenges and emo-tional dross between us had been burned away, and I was left with the pure gold of my love for her. It was beautiful. And excruciating. I was single parenting twin tween girls and trying to meet them in their grief. And let me tell you, single parenting is the worst. You have all the challenges of being single—the relational aloneness and surging sexual desires—without any of the characteristic blessings of singleness (freedom with time, more disposable income, fewer responsibilities). Those were the darkest days (years!) of my life. There were plenty of missteps in that season. Initially I sat in bed with my laptop, watching movies until I fell asleep night after night because I was unwill-ing to face the pain of an empty bed without the anesthesia of entertained distraction. I hoped a new relationship would bring healing. I'd never gone so long without a romantic con-nection with someone and didn't realize I'd been dependent on a woman to prop me up since junior high. In ways that are too long to tell, God brought me to the end of myself through that season and to a deeper relational place with him.

More than at any other time, I learned the truth that God wants to be our spouse. He meets us in our pain as our comforter. Like Paul, I learned that he truly is "the God of all comfort" (2 Corinthians 1:3). That sounds great, right? Here's what we don't like: the only way we learn this lesson is through suffering horribly and learning that he is sufficient. So, Paul explains, "For we do not want you to be unaware, brothers, of the affliction we experienced in Asia. For we were so utterly burdened beyond our strength that we despaired of life itself. Indeed, we felt that we had received the sentence of death. But that was to make us rely not on ourselves but on God who raises the dead" (2 Corinthians 1:8–9). Did you catch that? When Paul was pushed completely beyond his ability to endure, thinking death looked like a better option, God showed up to strengthen and restore. As he writes a little later, Jesus wants all of us to learn, "My grace is sufficient for you, for my power is made perfect in weakness" (12:9).

The only way we learn this is through our weakness. Our weakness and finitude puts us in touch with his infinite power, enabling us to taste the wonder of transcendence and see beyond this life with eyes of faith. That's why Paul writes that "this light momentary affliction is preparing for us an eternal weight of glory beyond all comparison" (2 Corinthians 4:17). *Light and momentary?!* He opens the letter talking about facing such fierce oppression that he despaired of life. But in Christ he experienced something so profound—a love surpassing knowledge (Ephesians 3:19) coupled with a hope so solid, "an eternal weight of glory"—that the most excruciating trial in this world became to him a mere "light momentary affliction." Paul discovered something more *real* in the comfort of God than the trials he suffered. (For a brief overview of Paul's sufferings, see 2 Corinthians 11:24–28.)

I want you to understand something of the road I walked, so you can grasp why this next Old Testament passage is so significant to me. I slowly emerged from the deep darkness of grief. I foreswore seeking a relationship and learned to lean on Jesus instead of a woman. I started facing my empty bedroom and went to bed at a reasonable time each night. (I even repainted it forest green and started turning it into a "man cave.") My girls and I settled into a new rhythm as a family of three. Though not entirely free from the challenge of frustrated sexual desire, I wasn't "burning with passion." I started praying about perhaps not remarrying. Truth be told, part of this was self-protective. I mean, what sane person would risk going through *that* again?! I remember receiving a ministry update from a friend about this time whose son had just gotten engaged. Someone surreptitiously captured the moment, so there was a photo of the young man down on one knee. As soon as I saw it, my immediate reaction was to audibly recoil: "Ugh." I had not totally sworn off dating and possible remarriage, and seeing someone happy in a relationship moving toward marriage hit me hard emotionally. A combination of pain and fear swept through me.

But then it happened—the fateful day when I taught a Sunday school class and was approached afterward by a young woman. She wanted to know if I was "on the market" because she had a friend who'd be perfect. I'd heard that line before. I had gone nearly a year without seeking a relationship, so I prayed about it for a month and felt free in the Spirit to follow up. We exchanged a couple witty emails back and forth, in which I disclosed my status as a widower pastor with twin girls (kind of an *Anne of Green Gables* character, except for the sex ministry), and then we had our first phone call, which lasted two hours. That was different! Long story short, we met and married in eight months. Our wedding song was Elvis's "Can't Help Falling in Love with You." That was my experience—I couldn't have made it stop even if I had wanted to. I was suddenly swept up in a romance that thrilled and consumed me.

Against the backdrop of the darkest season of my life, suddenly my heart reawakened. In the whirlwind of our early dating which turned quickly into our engagement and eager anticipation of our wedding day, I was blown away by these words, "For as a young man marries a young woman, so shall your sons marry you, and *as the bridegroom rejoices over the bride, so shall your God rejoice over you*" (Isaiah 62:5, emphasis added). I was struck afresh by the wonder of this verse: God created marriage and designed us with deep, romantic yearnings, so we would understand this fundamental truth. Everything you feel, the deep longing for connection, the desire to be "one flesh" with another, was built into you by God so that you'd have a small taste of his heart for you—his desire for a relationship with you, his longing for union with you, and his great anticipation for the last day when we'll sit down together for the wedding feast.

In that whirlwind season of new love, reawakened desire, and longing to be "one flesh" with Jennifer, it took my breath away to realize what I was experiencing was a drop in the Pacific Ocean of God's infinite heart for me . . . and you. Having talked for years about the truth that sex points to God, I was experiencing new depth of it in awe. He built marriage and romance into the fabric of his creation so that we would know this wondrous reality. During our engagement, I couldn't hug Jen close enough. Although sexual desire was certainly present, the yearning was more than that. I wanted to be *one* with her, interconnected in a way that was about union, not just sexual pleasure. This longing for a "reunion" between male and female, expressed through a physical union, though ultimately so much deeper, was really just a foretaste of a more wondrous union. Isaiah's description of the delight of an earthly bridegroom was my delight, but I was able to see it as derivative of the overjoyed longing of the ultimate Bridegroom.

Embracing Jesus as Your Lover

How would your relationship with God change if you pictured him as a lover, rather than a judge? Even if you feel more comfortable with God as your Father or Redeemer, how does it alter things to see him as your husband? What do you think is missing from your understanding if you do not have this crucial piece?

This unique perspective of "God with us" can revolutionize our relationship with him. Think about this example: A lover is excited to see you at the end of the day. He wants to hear about all the ins and outs of what's happening in your life. There are no mundane details! He's thinking about you when you're not together—anticipating your next rendezvous. A lover daydreams about you. You are "everything" to him. A lover is thoughtful. He is a student of *you*, wanting to learn what excites you and what delights you. Rejoicing in you, he wants you to rejoice. He wants to hear you laugh. I delight in my wife's laugh. I go to great lengths to make this happen—sometimes involving physical humor—usually to the annoyance of our older children who shockingly don't find me as funny. Why do I do this? I do it to delight her because I delight in her.

Unless we've experienced trauma that causes us to wall off our relationships with others, we all desperately want to be delighted in and desired. We want to know that someone is thinking about us and eager to be together again. This is a profoundly human experience because we are made in God's image to live in a relationship of love with him, a union for all eternity that is beyond our ability to comprehend. God's consistent use of marital imagery in the Bible is there to direct us to understand that our desires for intimacy and even sex are an invitation to worship. Even in our unsatisfied longings, he invites us to know his burning desire for us. He is eagerly looking forward to the coming wedding feast. And he's been waiting a long time! Jesus can't wait to sit down with us, his bride, at the wedding arranged by our Father since the foundation of the world. He can't wait to be united with you for all eternity!

CHAPTER 3

The Profound Mystery of Sex

Although God had been hinting in this direction for a few centuries, the marriage metaphor reaches its ultimate fruition with the incarnation of Jesus. Let's consider Paul's words in Ephesians 5:22–33, looking at the whole passage in context:

> Wives, submit to your own husbands, as to the Lord. For the husband is the head of the wife even as Christ is the head of the church, his body, and is himself its Savior. Now as the church submits to Christ, so also wives should submit in everything to their husbands.
>
> Husbands, love your wives, as Christ loved the church and gave himself up for her, that he might sanctify her, having cleansed her by the washing of water with the word, so that he might present the church to himself in splendor, without spot or wrinkle or any such thing, that she might be holy and without blemish. In the same way husbands should love their wives as their own bodies. He who loves his wife loves himself. For no one ever hated his own flesh, but nourishes and cherishes it, just as Christ does the church, because we are members of his body. *"Therefore a man shall leave his father and mother and hold fast to his wife, and the two shall become one flesh."* [Genesis 2:24] This mystery is profound, and I am saying that

it refers to Christ and the church. However, let each
one of you love his wife as himself, and let the wife see
that she respects her husband." (Ephesians 5:22–33,
emphasis added)

After discussing the roles of husbands and wives in marriage and reiterating the "one flesh" declaration of Genesis
2:24, Paul reaches an astonishing conclusion, "This mystery
is profound, and I am saying that it refers to Christ and the
church" (v. 32). This passage teaches that the whole point of
marriage, including the sexual expression within it, is for us
to understand our relationship to our Creator and Redeemer.

How should we process this "profound mystery"? To
begin, Paul provides guidance for husbands and wives because
he realizes marriage is difficult. Although he was personally
single (see 1 Corinthians 7:8), he saw the messy marriages in
the early church, especially among the pagan converts with
their particularly complicated sexual histories. But despite the
sexual failures of these early Christians, Paul is convinced that
God's design of marriage is powerful enough to transform
their lives. Even more shocking, Paul is convinced that the
story of Genesis, which was written ages before Jesus's earthly
life, actually speaks about Christ and the church.

A basic theological conviction about Scripture is that,
behind the human authors of the Bible, God's Spirit was at
work to inspire and direct God's revelation so that the biblical
authors wrote the Word of God. Along these lines, consider
Peter's declaration: "For no prophecy was ever produced by
the will of man, but men spoke from God as they were carried
along by the Holy Spirit" (2 Peter 1:21). Regarding Ephesians,
this means that Paul's claim that Genesis 2:24 refers to Christ
and the church is not an interpretive innovation or a rhetorical
flourish. Rather, when God established the institution of marriage at the creation of the world, he anticipated Paul penning
those lines! Marriage was created to reveal his own desire for

relationship with his people that would one day be fulfilled in the union between Christ and the church. Although hinted at throughout the Old Testament, the ultimate revelation of this mystery of marriage was "on hold," waiting to reach the climactic point in redemptive history when the wonder would finally be revealed in Christ, the ultimate Bridegroom.

Think about John 1:14: "The Word became flesh and dwelt among us . . ." These are some of the most familiar words in the New Testament. For centuries the Jewish people had longed, in various ways, for a deliverer who would rescue them from foreign oppressors and usher in a new age of righteousness and peace, but no one anticipated the incarnation of God *himself.* The early Christian belief that the Messiah of Israel was also the incarnate God of Israel—who not only shared human flesh but succumbed to a shameful death for his beloved—rocked Jewish monotheistic sensibilities. There was no way the Creator of the universe would become a creature! The polytheistic Greeks, with so many gods taking on flesh for pleasure (or vindictive mischief), had no category for the glorious uniqueness of the incarnation. But Jesus, the One through whom all things were made, humbled himself and fully embraced our humanity (see John 1:3; Colossians 1:16; Philippians 2:5–7). This is the scandal and beauty of the Incarnation.

What was the point of the Incarnation? "God with us"— the meaning of the name Immanuel (see Matthew 1:23). God entering into our experience. In Jesus, heaven and earth come together, so that he might "reconcile to himself all things" (Colossians 1:20) and "unite all things in him" (Ephesians 1:10). This means that union with Christ is at the heart of the gospel! In much of the American church, this holistic under-standing of the gospel has been lost. Instead, we (rightly) talk of atonement for our sins, but often we miss the bigger picture of what forgiveness of sins is *for.* Both of the aforementioned passages address the atonement because it is the absolutely critical foundation that makes union possible. But *union* with

Christ—sharing in his life—is the point! At the center of the gospel is God's reconciling love in Christ, which reestablishes our broken relationship with him and brings us to share the life of God "*in* Christ." (This is Paul's favorite phrase, which he uses over eighty times, to describe what it means to be a Christian.)

Jesus sums this up beautifully at the end of what is called his high priestly prayer:

> I do not ask for these only, but also for those who will believe in me through their word, that they may all be one, just as you, Father, are in me, and I in you, *that they also may be in us*, so that the world may believe that you have sent me. The glory that you have given me I have given to them, *that they may be one even as we are one, I in them and you in me*, that they may become perfectly one, so that the world may know that you sent me and loved them even as you loved me. Father, I desire that they also, whom you have given me, may be with me where I am, to see my glory that you have given me because you loved me before the foundation of the world. O righteous Father, even though the world does not know you, I know you, and these know that you have sent me. I made known to them your name, and I will continue to make it known, *that the love with which you have loved me may be in them, and I in them.*" (John 17:20–26, emphasis added)

Jesus's prayer suggests that we are ushered into the ultimate inner circle. Our union with Christ is the adoption into the extended family of the Godhead. Because union with Christ is at the center, marriage as a "one flesh" relationship provides a poignant metaphor to describe the wonder of our relationship with Jesus. Although the marriage metaphor was used in the Old Testament to describes God's relationship with Israel, it becomes much richer and explicit at the Incarnation.

Jesus as the Bridegroom

In the "fullness of time" when Jesus arrives on the scene, God's people behold the Bridegroom in the flesh at last. John the Baptist is the first to make the comparison between Jesus as the Bridegroom and the people as his bride. When John's disciples are concerned because Jesus is baptizing people and the crowds are now flocking to him, John patiently replies, "The one who has the bride is the bridegroom. The friend of the bridegroom, who stands and hears him, rejoices greatly at the bridegroom's voice. Therefore this joy of mine is now complete. He must increase, but I must decrease" (John 3:29–30). Not looking for personal glory, John delights to see Jesus exalted. He rejoices like a best man watching his childhood friend marry the woman of his dreams. Jesus also used parables to reorient the marriage imagery between God and Israel placing himself as the Bridegroom. In Matthew 22:1–14, he compares the kingdom of heaven to a king giving a wedding feast for his son. When those who are invited ignore the feast, the doors are flung wide in invitation to all who will come, for the king is looking for people to celebrate the wedding of his son.

Likewise, when challenged because his disciples did not fast, Jesus replied, "Can the wedding guests fast while the bridegroom is with them? As long as they have the bridegroom with them, they cannot fast. The days will come when the bridegroom is taken away from them, and then they will fast in that day" (Mark 2:19–20).[1] Do you hear what he is saying? The Bridegroom has come at last! This is a time for feasting and celebration. Although not evident to the masses at that point, the twelve disciples would eventually become the leaders of the twelve tribes of a newly constituted Israel—a people which, together with believing Gentiles, would now become the church, the bride of Christ.

The account of Jesus and the Samaritan woman in John 4:1–22 is a beautiful instance of an invitation to an outsider to join in the bridal party of the Son of God. The fact that Jesus meets the woman alone at a well is powerfully evocative. Who else meets at a well? Remember the prayerful journey of Abraham's servant that culminated at a well in a "chance" encounter with Rebekah, who consented to return with him to marry Isaac (Genesis 24). It was also at a well that Jacob met Rachel and instantly fell head over heels for her, willing to work years for her hand in marriage (Genesis 29). Fleeing Egypt, Moses rescued the daughters of Jethro from hostile shepherds and met Zipporah his wife at a well (Exodus 2:16–21). In the Bible, a man and woman meeting at a well is something like a pre-betrothal scene. Jesus came to this Samaritan outcast to woo her as his bride.

These metaphors of wedding and bridegroom come into vivid clarity with Paul's declaration of the "profound mystery" in Ephesians 5:32. With Jesus's resurrection and ascension to glory, the official betrothal period had begun. The Bridegroom has gone away to prepare a place for his bride (John 14:1–3). As the firstborn of creation and the firstfruits of the resurrection (Colossians 1:15; 1 Corinthians 15:20), Jesus is preparing for the union that we will share with him fully in the new creation. Although shrouded in mystery, Scripture points to the hope of a remade cosmos in which "the marriage of the Lamb has come" and "the dwelling place of God is with man" (Revelation 19:7; 21:3). Through his resurrection, Jesus alone has passed through death and come out the other side into the experience of new creation. But he is committed to bringing us, his bride, to be with him there. The marriage metaphor casts Jesus's well-known promise of going ahead to prepare a place for us in a wonderful new light (John 14:1–3).

The Mysterious "Other"

In chapter 1, we looked at how the creation of Eve was the result of seeking an opposite helper, a mirror image to complement the man. Their bodies were fashioned to fit together like puzzle pieces, and we described this coming together as a reunion, the reintegration of the image of God, which in some sense had been pulled apart to create the two sexes. Although this image-bearing diversity of humanity reflects God's mysterious triunity as Father, Son, and Spirit, there are significant implications of this diversity for understanding our relationship with Jesus in terms of marriage.

Our "otherness" as male and female in marriage is incredibly important. God created opposite-sex marriage as a picture of this deeper reality. In earthly marriage, a husband and wife become one flesh with someone who is wholly other in anticipation of our ultimate union with Jesus. As our Creator-made-flesh, Jesus is *categorically different* from us! There is a vast gulf in what theologians call the Creator-creature distinction, the difference between God and humanity.[2] As the God-man, in one sense Jesus bridges the gap for our redemption: "Therefore he had to be made like his brothers in every respect, so that he might become a merciful and faithful high priest in the service of God, to make propitiation for the sins of the people" (Hebrews 2:17). At the same time, because he is God incarnate, Jesus remains infinitely beyond and above us: "He is the radiance of the glory of God and the exact imprint of his nature, and he upholds the universe by the word of his power. After making purification for sins, he sat down at the right hand of the Majesty on high, having become as much superior to angels as the name he has inherited is more excellent than theirs" (Hebrews 1:3; also see Philippians 2:9–11).

The point here is that the radical otherness between Jesus and his people is a foundational component of God's design for marriage. Remember, God established marriage at creation in anticipation of this ultimate revelation in Christ. Because it is often a challenge for men to separate the idea of marriage from the sexual roles within it, many men struggle with being the bride of Christ. But setting that concern aside for the moment, think about it this way: in marriage both sexes are given a tiny foretaste of the wonder of the coming union with Christ because both are united to one so very different than themselves. Husband and wife each uniquely experience this union with one who is *other* in heterosexual marriage. Just as the profound pleasure of sex points beyond itself, providing a glimpse of deep theological truth, so the intrinsic differences of the sexes reflects a far more wondrous union with the One who is infinitely other.

The deep truths behind God's design for heterosexual marriage demonstrate why the church needs to establish a positive theology of sex. The otherness of husband and wife, rooted in the proclamation that marriage is about Jesus and the church, is foundational to God's design. This understanding is crucial for teaching our kids about biblical morality and for explaining our faith to those who do not believe. For example, this is one reason that gay marriage does not conform to the pattern of Christ and the church. The metaphor God wants us to understand involves differences joined into unity. The picture of Christ and his church breaks down if the members of the couple share the same sex. Why does this matter? One of the arguments for blessing same-sex marriage in the church is that God really cares only about love and monogamy. On this logic, gender is immaterial. If God cares only about the "spiritual" aspects of a relationship (love and commitment), then the physical difference (gender) really does not matter.[3]

In a way, this argument dredges up an old debate in church history about the significance of the material world. Against the prominent idea in Western philosophy that the physical world is irrelevant, the church rightly affirmed the inherent goodness of creation. A right view of sexuality means understanding God is not ambivalent about the material world but rather delights in it. Against the relativizing of our created bodies, we must recover a belief that God indeed had a good plan for his world and that he is not taking back his original declaration that the world as he made it is "very good." The call to be united to a member of the opposite sex isn't an abstract command that's irrelevant compared to the commitment to monogamy. Rather, this command is absolutely central so that each member of a covenantal union has the experience of connection with one who is completely "other" even as our ultimate union is with One *categorically* other.

Covenant Promises

For many people today, even inside the church, reserving sex for marriage seems not only antiquated but nonsensical. Why does marriage matter? I have heard Christian millennials argue that sex is okay in their relationship because they are deeply committed to each other and probably headed for marriage but the institution is impractical at the moment because of grad school or some other reason. But they deeply love each other. This view understands one basic aspect of biblical sexuality—sex should be with a single person of the opposite gender in the context of a lifelong relationship—but it screens out the fundamental foundation for a sexual relationship: *communal, covenantal promises.* A couple is married, not because of their deep love for each other or once they've consummated the union with physical intimacy, but when they mutually make the promises "before God and these witnesses," forsaking all others and committing the rest of their lives to each other. These covenant promises are the foundation for marital union because marriage and sexuality point to our relationship with God.

One of the most important ways that marital sexuality reflects the deeper truth of our relationship with Jesus is that at its very foundation are *covenantal promises.* Our relationship

with God is rooted in the promises he made that actually pre-
date Genesis 1! Although Christians reject the idea of an eter-
nally preexistent soul—there was no *you* before your body was
created—nevertheless you were known by God from *before
the foundation of the world.* The glorious coming kingdom of
the new heavens and new earth was prepared from before the
foundation of the world (Matthew 25:34). You were chosen in
Christ to be holy and blameless from before the foundation of
the world (Ephesians 1:4). And your name was "written before
the foundation of the world in the book of life of the Lamb
who was slain" (Revelation 13:8). All this is to say, our relationship is based on God's promises and his commitment. And
understanding his character is really important here. Paul's
theologically dense introduction to his letter to Titus contains
a crucial truth: God "never lies" (Titus 1:2). The writer of
Hebrews takes it even further:

> For when God made a promise to Abraham, since he
> had no one greater by whom to swear, he swore by
> himself, saying, "Surely I will bless you and multiply
> you." And thus Abraham, having patiently waited,
> obtained the promise. For people swear by something
> greater than themselves, and in all their disputes an
> oath is final for confirmation. So when God desired to
> show more convincingly to the heirs of the promise the
> unchangeable character of his purpose, he guaranteed
> it with an oath, so that by two unchangeable things, in
> which it is impossible for God to lie, we who have fled
> for refuge might have strong encouragement to hold
> fast to the hope set before us. We have this as a sure
> and steadfast anchor of the soul, a hope that enters
> into the inner place behind the curtain, where Jesus
> has gone as a forerunner on our behalf, having become
> a high priest forever after the order of Melchizedek.
> (6:13–20)

This is a rich portion of Scripture, and we are going to barely scratch the surface. But it's important to note that God's commitment to us is rooted in his promises. God begins by making a promise to Abraham to bless the entire world through him (Genesis 12:1–3). I love that after God gave Abraham the promise, he went even farther and made an oath, swearing by himself because there was no one greater to swear by (see Genesis 22:15–18). God doubled down on his promise. He didn't need to make an oath. Because God does not lie, his single promise alone should have sufficed. But he is a loving God who knows the fears and weaknesses of his children. Despite our faith in Jesus, he knows we are prone to wander and that we regularly fail. He knows our propensity to question his goodness and faithfulness.

When my kids are surprised by my benevolence, my default is to be hurt or defensive. I want to say, "Why wouldn't you expect me to pay for your senior T-shirt (sports banquet, college application, or youth group activity), don't you know I'm generous?!" But this is not how God deals with us. He perfectly understands our weakness and tenderly meets us, making a promise and confirming with an oath, to bolster our frail faith and assure us of his utter devotion to us. Rather than taking it as a slight to his perfect character, he graciously accommodates our frailty—"For he knows our frame; he remembers that we are dust" (Psalm 103:14).

Our ultimate hope is that God is a covenantal, promise-keeping God. Marriage is a relationship based entirely on promises and public, binding oaths. The promises made between husband and wife to remain faithful, no matter what comes and to forsake all others, is a picture of God's incredible commitment to us. It is a dim reflection of the amazing reality that "neither death nor life, nor angels nor rulers, nor things present nor things to come, nor powers, nor height nor depth, nor anything else in all creation, will be able to separate us from the love of God in Christ Jesus our Lord" (Romans 8:38–39).

The covenantal blessings of marriage that include both the mundane, such as shared finances and household chores, and the glorious opportunity for rich *yada*—the deep knowing of another in which sex is part of the relational celebration—are all rooted in the promises made by the couple on their wedding day. The blessings of marriage are the result of committing to covenant promises because God wants to reveal something profound about his relationship to us. All the blessings of relationship with God—whose fullness we will not know until we see him face-to-face—flow to us because he has given us great and precious promises which are all yes and amen in Christ (see 2 Corinthians 1:20; 2 Peter 1:4).

For this reason, God intends the ecstasy of sexual pleasure to flow from publicly made covenantal promises. Strong emotions for one another are important but not sufficient to warrant sexual union. The good intention of lifelong fidelity is not enough. People do not need a "piece of paper" to prove their love for each other. The point is not getting a stamp of approval from the church or state. The issue is whether this couple is willing to make public promises committing their entire self and future to one another. Only this is good enough to merit the glory of godly sexuality because only this mirrors the radical commitment of our God who is zealous for us and longs for our sexual union to reflect his commitment of love made by promise and oath, ratified by his own blood.

Of course, there are practical implications to all this. Most good things in life take time and a lot of patience. This is especially true of our relationships. Making promises forces you to commit for the long haul. This is incredibly important because marriage is hard! I love the blunt honesty of the disciples. When Jesus reiterated that God's design for marriage is a lifelong commitment, they replied, "If such is the case of a man with his wife, it is better not to marry" (Matthew 19:10). More than a few newlyweds experience this jarring thought even before the end of their honeymoon, *Oh, no! What have*

I done? But promises compel us to the hard work of persever-
ance. I remember hitting a rough patch early in my first marriage, crying out to God one morning on the drive to work and
having a profound sense from the Spirit of needing to address
the issues. If not, they would *always* be a problem. For the rest
of my days. In this case, the public promises I made forced me
to commit to working on my marriage even when it was hard:
". . . in plenty and in want, in joy and in sorrow, in sickness
and in health."

But it is deeper than that. As image-bearers we are immor-
tal beings with a depth and splendor to discover. True *yada*,
deep knowing, takes decades of intimate conversations and
shared experiences. It grows as our lives intersect with others.
I long for more alone time with my wife. Life with two preschoolers and two high school students is very full. But the
truth is, I actually have more of Jennifer because her interactions with each of our children bring out different facets of
her personality. Not to mention her engagement with extended
family, neighbors, and church friends.[4]

And commitment to the long haul is critical for our sexual
relationship. Our culture derides monogamy as boring and
declares marriage as the death knell for good sex, but couples
committed to *yada* as a foundation for their marriage report
that their sexual relationship to each other has grown over the
years. As a couple knows each other and grows in learning the
mysterious other, there is an opportunity for deepening sexual
satisfaction. As in most aspects of the Christian life, it is "a
long obedience in the same direction"[5] that results in greater
fruit in the marriage bed.

A Jealous Lover

Consider this: God created humanity with a strong, romantic
impulse because he wants us to see his passionate love for us
behind it all. Back of the thrill we experience with falling in

love, he wants us to know his delight in having a relationship with us. If you are struggling in an emotionally distant marriage or are single and longing for romantic intimacy, Jesus wants you to know his longing for you in the pain of your unanswered desires. There is a reason why we are filled with deep romantic stirrings and a longing to connect with another. We have a yearning for completion. But at its basic level, this longing is a reflection of our inborn desire for union with God and of Jesus's heart for his beloved bride.

Falling in love is one of the most glorious human experiences. (Unless you know the far deeper sweetness of love that has endured the years, through trial and tribulation, maturing into something far more substantial and glorious!) The work of artists and poets span the millennia in praise of this exquisite experience. And falling in love is uniquely *human*, an aspect of our image-bearing. Nearly all creatures mate in some way. The male and female binary permeates the created order—even in plant life! Among mating creatures, there is usually some ritual that connects sexual desirability in the physical realm. Whether it is male bison head-butting to prove to the females their superior strength or the outrageous mating exploits of the tropical birds of paradise (never ceasing to produce regales of laughter from the whole family when we watch *Planet Earth*), the animal kingdom often employs some special behavior to seek a mate. But only humans have a romantic drive to connect emotionally and spiritually. This deep longing is another reflection of our image-bearing, and coupled with our creativity, it has resulted in an endless flow of artistic expression throughout the ages.

We see this passion in the Bible's description of God's heart for us. How do you feel about God's jealousy? In several key places in the Old Testament he is described as a "jealous God" (Exodus 20:5; Deuteronomy 5:9). He is jealous because he wants an exclusive relationship with us, just like a spouse. Describing how passions for things of this world lead to enmity with God, James tells us, "He yearns jealously over the spirit that he has made to dwell in us" (James 4:5). Now, most of us see jealousy as an extreme negative. This is *not* a characteristic we want in a friend, let alone a spouse. Why? A jealous person is typically excessively needy and distrusting. Jealousy usually results from real or perceived deficiencies. As a result, insecurity abounds. Ruled by fear of losing the relationship to another who's more desirable, the jealous person is desperate for control. The posture is inherently self-protective.

The contrast with God's jealousy could not be more dramatic. There is no deficiency or neediness in God. As we looked at in chapter 1, God exists from all eternity in perfect trinitarian harmony and love; he didn't create humanity in the desperate attempt to stave off divine loneliness or in response to some other personal defect. He created the universe out of the overflow of his fullness of relational love. C. S. Lewis's description is great: "God, who needs nothing, loves into existence wholly superfluous creatures in order that He may love and perfect them."[6] Do you see the amazing difference? He is jealous as one who only and always has *your best* in view. His divine contentedness means he is not looking for you to fill or satisfy him in any way. Although our affections glorify him, and he is zealous to receive them, he does not *need* them.

So, God's jealousy is completely distinct from human jealousy. He is not insecure or needy. Relationally, he wants to bless us. God's jealousy stems from his role as the Creator—he knows what is best for his creatures. His jealousy is rooted in wanting an *exclusive* relationship with his people in which we live in the dependent love we were created to experience. And this is a significant reason why marriage as an exclusive relationship is the only context for sexual expression.

The exclusivity of marriage points to our exclusive relationship with Jesus. God designed the emotional and physical fidelity of marriage to reflect our absolute spiritual fidelity to Jesus. The call for a husband and wife to forsake all others and

be bound together in a lifelong union echoes the command that
we should have no other gods before him (Exodus 20:3). Our
relational fidelity in marriage points to our spiritual fidelity to
Jesus, who will one day return as our ultimate Bridegroom.
Although what this means is a "profound mystery" (Ephesians
5:32) and is part of our sharing in an "eternal weight of glory
beyond all comparison" (2 Corinthians 4:17), which "no eye
has seen, nor ear heard, nor the heart of man imagined" (1
Corinthians 2:9), marriage stands as a signpost. When the
emotional and spiritual oneness are at their earthly best and
a couple enters into the marriage bed, celebrating their oneness with the delight of pleasuring each other, there is a tiny
foretaste of the life to come. God's jealousy for our exclusive
spiritual affection is a foundation for creating the lifelong, covenant bond of marriage.

Reflecting the jealous heart of our God, husbands and
wives should remain zealous for the affections of their spouse
as the years wind on. It is easy for spouses to become compla-
cent in their pursuit of one another, and cool in their jealousy
for cultivating their relationship. Pursuit of career, hobbies, or
other friendships impinge on nurturing the marriage. One of
the greatest dangers to a deepening *yada* is not rival human
lovers, but complacency. What steps can you take to quicken
your jealousy for your spouse? Are you committed to dating
each other? Are you looking for small and big ways to surprise
and bless your spouse? Are you actively seeking to bond in
your marriage through physical intimacy? Are you committed
to pursuing spiritual and emotional *yada*? As we reflect on the
jealous love God has pledged to us, may we be drawn more
deeply into embodying that love by jealously nurturing our
own covenant marriages.

CHAPTER 4

Sexual Pleasure Reveals
a God of Delight

Christianity has always been rooted in the goodness of the creation. As we have seen, God created a physical world and declared it to be "very good" (Genesis 1:31). This is important because trends in both Eastern and Western philosophies have undermined the physical world in favor of a purely spiritual existence.

Years ago, on a long flight from Philadelphia to San Diego, I had a conversation with a college freshman who was exploring Buddhism. He expressed the common idea that if we distill every religion to their essence, they're essentially the same. I challenged him with the radical difference of Christianity against Buddhism in their most basic elements. Rather than eternal nothingness, the Bible begins "In the beginning, God . . ." (Genesis 1:1). Far from rejecting the physical, Christianity embraces the material world with an ultimate hope of a re-created cosmos beyond our wildest imagination. In fact, "God so loved the world" (John 3:16) that he personally entered our physical existence, experiencing the full breadth of human emotion and enduring profound suffering, in order to reconcile us, because the uniqueness of every individual and personal relationship matters.

As mentioned in the last chapter, this fundamental biblical doctrine came under assault early in church history. Various New Testament passages express concern to hold on to a faithful perspective about the goodness of creation. For example, Paul warns against false teachers who are challenging what food and drink are permissible, pushing asceticism and "severity to the body" (Colossians 2:16–23). Marriage and sexuality were also being undermined, which prompted several writers to be very clear about its high place and blessing (see 1 Corinthians 7:1–5; Hebrews 13:4).

From the beginning, the Bible affirms that our bodies are included in the "very good" of creation. Consider the creation of Adam (Genesis 2:7). It is significant that first God formed his body and then breathed life into him. Some people refer to humanity as "embodied souls." Given the ordering of God's actions, it's actually more accurate to describe us as "ensouled bodies." Although this may strike you as hairsplitting, it is important. The idea of an embodied soul exalts the one over the other. This fosters the perspective that an eternal soul was joined temporarily with a physical body that will one day be shunted aside when our liberated souls ascend to heaven. But against such a view, the Bible teaches that our bodies are integral to who we are. And the biblical hope is a future bodily resurrection in a re-created cosmos. God's good design for a physical world will stretch into eternity.

The goodness of our bodies is loudly heralded in 1 Corinthians 6:12–20, a passage focused on warning against sexual immorality. But the primary reason given is that "the body" is meant "for the Lord, and the Lord for the body" (v. 13). This was a shocking statement in the first century. The fact the world groans under the curse, in need of redemption, does not negate God's good work in creation. Written at a time when much of Greek philosophy denigrated physical existence, the New Testament was radically countercultural. Going against the tide of Platonism that viewed the physical world as weak and superficial and would be eventually transcended by a purely spiritual existence, Christianity taught the goodness of the physical world and that the hope for humanity wasn't a disembodied spiritual eternity but a new heavens and earth. The current pain of life in the physical world expresses a yearning for the physical redemption that began in Christ's resurrection and that will one day encompass the entire cosmos (see Romans 8:18–25). The New Testament remains unashamedly positive about our physical bodies, including our sexuality.

The God of Pleasure

Corresponding to the goodness of creation is God's character as the Creator who delights in the pleasure of his creatures. He is the Giver of good gifts. This is hard for us to embrace for at least two reasons.

First, we continue to hear the hissing voice, "Did God actually say, 'You shall not eat from any tree of the garden'?" (Genesis 3:1). The enemy called into question the goodness of God's character. Ever since, we've struggled to believe that God truly wants to bless us and give us good gifts. Several years ago, I read Psalm 36 and had a visceral reaction when I came to verse 8: "They feast on the abundance of your house, and you give them drink from the river of your delights." My response: *Really?! River of delights?* I was surprised by my involuntary reaction to such a sweet declaration by God. Fortunately, I was at a point in my relationship with God that talking with him about his Word was integral to reading the Bible. I confessed my unbelief and asked for more grace to truly know him. I asked to know this experientially, and for him to grant me more of his Spirit so I would trust when I was *not* feeling it. In what ways is this true for you? Why do you doubt that God wants us to delight in pleasure? For most of us, the hook of Satan's initial deception is set deep.

Second, pleasure can sweep us away. Because our appetites easily overwhelm us, Greek philosophy spurned the physical and religions like Buddhism denigrate emotion and pleasure. And this is why the New Testament contrasts wanton sexuality with the presence of the Holy Spirit. The goal of the Christian life is to live with self-control, a fruit of the Spirit's presence within us. God created us with these desires and declared them to be "very good." But I understand the temptation. A good friend's wife makes *really good* cookies that he's dubbed, "bars of sin." When a tray is in front of him, he's prone to go way beyond the appropriate serving size.

In *Perelandra*, the second book of C. S. Lewis's Space Trilogy, Dr. Ransom landed on Venus, an unfallen planet. After an exhausting physical ordeal, he came upon an exotic fruit (it's Venus, after all!). Ransom experienced profound pleasure as he drained the gourd. The pleasure was so exquisite that Ransom realized that once this fruit was tasted, wars would be fought to attain it. As he finished, his immediate temptation was to grab another gourd, but he instinctively realized he must not. (Remember, it's an unfallen world, so he received a greater measure of grace.) He had eaten and was satisfied. The appropriate response was to give thanks for the pleasure, enjoy the current experience of satiation, and get some much-needed rest.[1] All of us can identify with the desire to grab another, to repeat a pleasure we've enjoyed. The problem is not with the pleasure itself but with our inability to know when to stop. With certain pleasures, our appetite becomes insatiable. As one of life's sweetest pleasures, sex is an area where humanity tends to go off the rails big time.

Instead of gratefully receiving God's gifts and finding our contentment in him, we often turn to the pleasures of this world with a voracious appetite. But as God's image-bearers, our souls were created for the infinite satisfaction that only he can provide. The problem is not that our physical desires (including sexual desire) are actually insatiable. But they become enlarged and corrupted when not framed within a life oriented toward the singular love of God. Our bodies have desires for finite things, but our souls were made to need, seek, and love our *infinite* God. When our souls take guidance from our bodily desires, we end up trying to satiate the infinitely deep, soul yearnings with the finite stuff of this world. This is what the Bible calls idolatry. As Saint Augustine famously wrote, "You have made us for yourself, and our heart is restless until it rests in you."[2] Like all good gifts, sex invites us to see the goodness of the Giver behind the gift. In that way, all pleasures invite us to deeper worship. Far from shunning pleasure, the Christian faith invites us to embrace pleasure and to worship God through it all.

He wants us to experience pleasure without guilt and to know contentment, not constant yearning. Psalm 36 invites us to revel in God's goodness, to exclaim, "How precious is your steadfast love, O God!" (v. 7). Ponder this amazing truth: it was God's idea to put all those nerve endings in our genitals. God crafted the orgasm and declared it to be very good! The intense pleasure is a sign of God's blessing and delight in sexuality. This is incredibly important because it communicates something crucial about God: he is a God of pleasure! Pleasure, in all its glorious manifestations, was God's idea at creation, flowing from the immense pleasure he experiences within himself. This means taste buds are his invention. We delight in chocolate because God spoke taste into existence. The glorious spectrum of colors and our ability to see them, this beautiful world with all its breathtaking visual wonders— all this is his design. He created hearing so our hearts could soar to a Mozart concerto and delight in the birds warbling outside the window on a spring morning. Implicit through it all is that our God is a God of pleasure.

God Delights in Sex

God's delight in pleasure includes our sexuality. Do you remember the very first command given to God's newly created humanity? "Be fruitful and multiply and fill the earth . . ." (Genesis 1:28). John Freeman's paraphrase of this verse: "Have sex and lots of it!"[3] What an astounding command! The Bible is a big book and there is a lot God wants to say to us, but incredibly this is where he starts. His first order of business was to invite Adam and Eve into the blissful experience of sexuality necessary for multiplication.

Now, I do not want to overstate the case. This command, with the accompanying sexual expression, is inextricably linked with procreation and our call to rule over the earth as God's stewards. God has a goal beyond Adam and Eve's pleasure with each other. But it is inescapable that from the very moment of creation, sex is at the forefront of God's calling on his people. It was by the means of this pleasure that the creation mandate is fulfilled. Obviously, procreation is important, but consider: if this was the only purpose to sexuality it would have made more sense to create us asexual, like self-splitting amoebas. Or we could've been patterned after the hydra and budded new offspring, perhaps sprouting out of our shoulders at appropriately-timed intervals. (If it was up to me, we would've been spared the *years* of 24-7 childcare!) Given the challenges facing couples in their sexuality, this might have been a far more effective way to "be fruitful and multiply and fill the earth." Clearly, God had much more in view than procreation when he designed our sexuality. But stop and consider the wonder of that first command to humanity. From the very first page, the Bible is clearly positive about sex.

Similarly, it is significant that Jesus's first miracle took place at a wedding in Cana (John 2:1–11), in which Jesus revealed his glory through a ridiculously extravagant transformation of over 120 gallons of water into excellent wine. Jesus enters into the sweet celebration of this couple's union and goes way over the top to bless it.

The New Testament consistently affirms the goodness of marital sexuality, a sentiment simply and beautifully stated in Hebrews 13:4, "Let marriage be held in honor among all, and let the marriage bed be undefiled, for God will judge the sexually immoral and adulterous." This was written at a time when rumblings had already begun in the fledgling church, echoing the antiphysical teaching of Greek philosophy. Countering this, the Bible calls us to honor marriage and sexuality as a fundamental good.

One of the challenges to a positive perspective of sexuality is that many New Testament passages seem only to rebuke sexual immorality. But many also contain wondrous affirmations of sex. Consider 1 Thessalonians 4:3–4: "For this is the will of God, your sanctification: that you abstain from sexual immorality; that each one of you know how to control his own body in holiness and honor." In the cultural context in which Paul wrote these words, it was an astounding statement that there is a way to steward our body sexually "in holiness and honor," since much of Greek philosophy denigrated the body. And it is even more robust than it appears on the surface as many scholars have argued that the Greek word translated as "body" would be more accurately rendered "vessel," likely a euphemism for the sexual organs.[4]

In the philosophical context of Thessalonica when Paul penned this letter, this was an amazing statement. There is a way to steward our sexuality that is holy! This is shocking even to our twenty-first-century ears because too often guilt and shame are associated with sex. In Christ that guilt is removed, and the redemption of sex means we can experience *holy sexuality*. We need to take a step back and remember that to be holy is to be "set apart." In the tabernacle and temple, all the objects used for worship went through a ritual to be made holy. They were "set apart" for the glorious use of worshiping God. Holy sexuality means a sexuality that demonstrates we are set apart for him. Even our sexuality is "in Christ."

Sex is also honorable. In Christ, sex is no longer characterized by shame. When God looks at a husband and wife in the midst of their intimate revelry, he rejoices in the holy and honorable activity taking place before him. Christianity honors our sexuality and teaches us that God delights in it. God is calling married couples to have holy, honorable sex. In this way, sexuality in marriage should facilitate deeper worship, enabling us to praise God for the gift of our spouse and rejoice in his good gift of sexuality.

Now, I'm aware that some of my single readers have just picked the book back up from the floor, where it landed after hitting the wall. You too are invited to be holy and honorable in your sexuality. Rather than through sexual expression, it is primarily through "control" that you demonstrate a sexuality that is "set apart," characterized by honor rather than shame. Obviously, this is an incredibly hard calling! But it is so critical. (There's a reason why I've devoted a later chapter to single sexuality.) Our surrounding culture denigrates your decision to follow Jesus in this amazing way. Your obedience demonstrates to a watching world that there is something sweeter than sex to live for. Our world desperately chases sexual satisfaction, but having turned sex into an idol, they are racing on a hamster wheel. Your life, despite the challenges of chastity, boldly proclaims the truth of the risen King and the hope of his eternal kingdom to the principalities and powers of this dark age (see Ephesians 3:10).

Echoes of Eden

There is a glory to sexuality because it is both a signpost pointing ahead to the coming paradise and a reminder of the paradise lost. Consider the final description of creation immediately before the account of the fall: "Therefore a man shall leave his father and his mother and hold fast to his wife, and they shall become one flesh. *And the man and his wife were both naked and were not ashamed*" (Genesis 2:24–25, emphasis added). This is the last, fading image of humanity as God designed us free of sin. It is a blissful glimpse far removed from our experience of life, which is tinged with guilt and shame. This is why marital sexuality is so important, for in marital intimacy where husband and wife are naked and unashamed with each other, we hear echoes of Eden.

The Song of Solomon is the most robust proclamation of the bliss of human sexuality in the Bible. In fact, the language is so frank in its depiction of sensual desire that the church has often shied away from teaching it as a celebration of erotic romance. Through much of church history this book was read solely as an allegory about Jesus and the church. The concern with a purely allegorical approach is that it may reinforce a dualistic view of the world that impugns our physical natures. This mode of interpretation grew through the medieval period as Christian thinkers continued to be deeply influenced by Greek philosophy. But, as we have seen, both the Old and New Testament affirm the goodness of our created bodies. Accordingly, the Song of Solomon, with its vivid rendering of sexual desire, should not be a problem for Christian readers.

Rather than interpreting the Song of Solomon as an extended narrative poem with a cohesive, single story line, most scholars understand it to be a collection of individual love poems.[5] As such, they invite us to focus on the images present in each scene, rather than trying to work out a coherent narrative to the entire work. These passages reveal a God who delights in a couple's physical intimacy. This form of ancient Near Eastern love poetry was important enough to make it into the canon of Holy Scripture. Contrasting the church's historic fearful approach to sexuality, this little book is a celebration of human sexuality.

The Song of Solomon contains sweet depictions of the naked and unashamed bliss of created paradise. So, the intimacy of the man and woman is frequently described as happening outside in a garden setting, reflecting a return to Eden. Read these lines: "Our couch is green; the beams of our house are cedar; our rafters are pine" (1:16–17). This portrayal envisions a couple sprawling together in lush green grass, staring up at the boughs of trees interlacing above. Spring is in the air, the time for love, so the man gives the invitation for her to come out with him into the beauty: "Arise, my love, my beautiful one, and come away, for behold, the winter is past; the rain is over and gone. The flowers appear on the earth, the time of singing has come, and the voice of the turtledove is heard in our land. The fig tree ripens its figs, and the vines are in blossom; they give forth fragrance. Arise, my love, my beautiful one, and come away" (2:10–13).

Combining the images of the woman as a garden and the garden as a location for intimacy, the woman declares, "My beloved has gone down to his garden to the beds of spices, to graze in the gardens and to gather lilies. I am my beloved's and my beloved is mine; he grazes among the lilies" (6:2–3). A climactic poem in the collection describes the couple stealing away to the vineyard to make love: "Come, my beloved, let us go out into the fields and lodge in the villages; let us go out early to the vineyards and see whether the vines have budded, whether the grape blossoms have opened and the pomegranates are in bloom. There I will give you my love" (7:11–12). Marital sexuality at its best is a picture of paradise, a return to the sheer bliss of creation. This is profoundly true because sex was designed to point us to God and our union with Christ.

In addition to the garden imagery associated with intimate activity, the Song of Solomon contains bold proclamations of naked sexuality. Although there are several occasions where the couple comments specifically on each other's bodies, in two passages each of them delights in the other from head to toe (5:10–16; 7:1–5). We need to see this. The Bible's approach to sex isn't "Turn out the lights! Quick! Under the covers!" As the man and woman praise each other's form, it's as if they're standing outside, stark naked in the bright sunlight, an arm's length apart, reveling in the wonder of the bare body before each of them. And this includes frank delight in each other's sexuality.

You need to know something: English Bible translators tend to make technically accurate, but very safe, interpretive decisions when translating certain passages of the Song of Solomon. Using metaphors from everyday life to describe the naked bodies of husband and wife, the content is not titillating, but it is profoundly sensual, making clear that we can talk frankly about sex in ways that are "holy and honorable." Although contemporary wisdom generally holds that men are more visually wired than women, this woman rejoices to behold her man's body. In the most vivid description she exclaims, "His body is polished ivory, bedecked with sapphires" (5:14). Many scholars argue this would be better rendered loins or even refers directly to his penis.[6] She describes his sexual organs as valuable and precious to her. Similarly, the man passionately describes the woman beginning with her delicately-sandaled feet and moving upward. Between his description of her "rounded thighs" as jewels crafted by a master's hand and her belly as a "heap of wheat, encircled with lilies," the English Standard Version has "Your navel is a rounded bowl that never lacks mixed wine" (7:1–2). Given the way the man's eyes sweep upward and his poignant description, scholars argue that he's at least euphemistically describing her vagina.[7]

Describing her figure as a palm tree and her breasts as its fruit, the man boldly declares, "I say I will climb the palm tree and lay hold of its fruit. Oh may your breasts be like clusters of the vine, and the scent of your breath like apples, and your mouth like the best wine" (7:8–9). There is an unashamed glee in his sexual longing as he anticipates finding contentment in his mate. Similarly, the father of Proverbs 5:19 exhorts his son concerning the marriage bed: "Let her breasts fill you at all times with delight; be intoxicated always in her love." Part of God's design for sexuality is thus for a husband to be filled with "delight" in his wife's breasts.[8] Similarly, the woman in the Song of Solomon delights to embrace her man to her bosom: "My beloved is to me a sachet of myrrh that lies between my breasts" (1:13).

Since the fall, humanity has lived with a sexuality in need of redemption. That means all of us have some level of shame associated with our sexuality. These passages are vital to sexual redemption, inviting us to experience anew being naked and unashamed in marriage. The marriage bed is a reminder of the bliss of Eden, but even more, it's a foretaste of an infinitely greater union. In Christ, there is no shame in marital sexuality, and he invites us to dive deep into this pleasure and marvel at the profound mystery it portends.

The Goodness of Desire

Because the fall has distorted our sexuality, sexual desire gets a bad rap. But despite repeated warnings against immorality, the Bible celebrates sex in its God-ordained context. Consider again the invitation in Proverbs to husbands: "Be intoxicated always in her love." God wants married couples to be drunk with sexual delight in one another. The Hebrew word carries connotations of "wandering off," getting lost. God wants spouses to be lost with each other in their sexual relationship. You know what it's like to be with an infatuated couple oblivious to everyone around them, lost in their puppy love. God is saying married couples should experience this enraptured delight, specifically through their sexuality. Although it will change over time, the intoxicated elation of your sexual relationship and love for each other should remain.

In fact, our longings are described as a hunger and thirst, so sexual fulfillment is most frequently compared to satiating our appetites with food and drink. The Song of Solomon frequently depicts sexual intimacy by using language of pleasurable consumption, expressing how a sexual relationship satisfies these desires like a lush banquet. In one passage, the woman declares, "As an apple tree among the trees of the forest, so is my beloved among the young men. With great delight I sat in his shadow, and his fruit was sweet to my taste. He brought me to the banqueting house, and his banner over me was love" (2:3–4). Sexual love is better than the richness of wine and giddiness of intoxication (see 1:2, 4; 4:10; 5:1; 7:9).

In this feast, the man and woman entice and satisfy each other. She invites him, "Let my beloved come to his garden, and eat its choicest fruits" (4:16). The man delights to reply, "I came to my garden, my sister, my bride, I gathered my myrrh with my spice, I ate my honeycomb with my honey, I drank my wine with my milk" (5:1). As mentioned above, he compares her breasts to coconuts, and he climbs the palm tree to seize them (7:8–9). When he recounts her mouth is like the best wine, she rejoins, "It goes down smoothly for my beloved, gliding over lips and teeth. I am my beloved's, and his desire is for me" (vv. 9–10). The intensity of sexual desire is a hunger that marital sexuality is intended to satisfy. Hear the incredible sweetness in the expression of their love: "Your lips drip nectar, my bride; honey and milk are under your tongue" (4:11). He has an appetite that only passionately kissing this woman will satisfy!

Further, the woman's body itself is depicted as a garden to sate hunger and a well to quench thirst: "A garden locked is my sister, my bride, a spring locked, a fountain sealed. Your shoots are an orchard of pomegranates with all choicest fruits, henna with nard, nard and saffron, calamus and cinnamon, with all trees of frankincense, myrrh and aloes, with all choice spices—a garden fountain, a well of living water, and flowing streams from Lebanon" (4:12–15). Similarly, Proverbs describes a man's wife as a refreshing fountain of water to quench her husband's thirst: "Drink water from your own cistern, flowing water from your own well. . . . Let your fountain be blessed, and rejoice in the wife of your youth (5:15, 18). As the Song of Solomon makes clear, God intends lovers to find their intimacy, specifically each other's bodies, *deeply satisfying* to their sexual desires.

Women Like Sex Too

While Proverbs 5 describes the wife as a fountain, an invitation to be refreshed and fulfilled, it also contains a stark warning to protect the integrity of the marital union so that a wife is not left deprived and yearning for other suitors. "Should your springs be scattered abroad, streams of water in the streets? Let them be for yourself alone, and not for strangers with you" (vv. 16–17). Notice that the Bible is unashamedly positive about a woman's sexual desire and actually commands husbands to satisfy their wives! Even in our day, female sexual desire is often downplayed, especially in the church. I recently heard a woman describe her experience as a teen in the evangelical purity movement. The intense sexual desire of teenage boys was discussed at length as part of this teaching, but there was no admission or affirmation of sexual desire among young women. They were simply told they needed to protect young men who were unable to control their rampaging sexuality. The responsibility of safeguarding sexual purity was thus placed on the women's shoulders, with no acknowledgement of their own emerging desires, while young men were implicitly taught that they were not capable of exercising responsibility for themselves or capable of encouraging purity among their sisters. Diminishing the responsibility of young men contributes to struggles with self-control and encourages them to see their own sexual failures—including, tragically, acts of sexual aggression—as the fault of women. Against such a sad distortion, the Bible teaches that men and women have good sexual desires that each must steward with wisdom and godly self-control.

For many women this distortion increases their shame over their sexuality, especially when they wrestle with sexual sin. Again, the Bible is often more honest than the church. This is why Paul *commands* husbands and wives to take sexual gratification seriously: "The husband should give to his wife her conjugal rights, and likewise the wife to her husband. For the wife does not have authority over her own body, but the husband does. Likewise the husband does not have authority over his own body, but the wife does. Do not deprive one another" (1 Corinthians 7:3–5). Unlike the evangelical teen purity movement, Scripture acknowledges a woman's desire and her "right" to be sexually satisfied in marriage.

This was revolutionary in the first century, and it remains so today. Because most men are able to climax sexually without difficulty, while women take more time and devoted attention to climax, a woman's sexual satisfaction is anything but guaranteed in marriage. The Bible is leveling the playing field, saying a husband must be committed to serving his wife this way, not cheating or defrauding her of this "conjugal right." In an age when Christianity is seen as regressive and sexist, passages like this invite us to consider how the Bible's ethic affirms women and can lead to marriages that flourish.

The Song of Solomon highlights the woman's sexual desire even more distinctly than the man's, all without shame. The book begins with the woman's excited invitation, "Let him kiss me with the kisses of his mouth! For your love is better than wine" (1:2). As she describes entering the "banqueting house" of their love she implores, "Sustain me with raisins; refresh me with apples, for I am sick with love" (2:4–5). She is weak in the knees with her desire and needs the sustenance that she'll only receive when "His left hand is under my head, and his right hand embraces me!" (v. 6).

In two different poems, the woman recounts awakening in the night, filled with sexual yearning.

> On my bed by night
> I sought him whom my soul loves;
>   I sought him, but found him not.
> I will rise now and go about the city,
>   in the streets and in the squares;
> I will seek him whom my soul loves.
>   I sought him, but found him not.
> The watchmen found me
>   as they went about in the city.
> "Have you seen him whom my soul loves?"
> Scarcely had I passed them
>   when I found him whom my soul loves.
> I held him, and would not let him go
>   until I had brought him into my mother's house,
>   and into the chamber of her who conceived me. (3:1–4)

Filled with longing, She seeks desperately, and finally finding him, she clings tightly and will not let go until she's satisfied. The description of bringing him into her own mother's bridal chamber is pregnant imagery in every sense.

In an even more poignant poem, the woman experiences an erotic dream and wakes in the night, filled with sexual longing for her man, only to be left unsatisfied.

> I slept, but my heart was awake.
> A sound! My beloved is knocking.
> "Open to me, my sister, my love,
>   my dove, my perfect one,
> for my head is wet with dew,
>   my locks with the drops of the night."

I had put off my garment;
    how could I put it on?
I had bathed my feet;
    how could I soil them?
My beloved put his hand to the latch,
    and my heart was thrilled within me.
I arose to open to my beloved,
    and my hands dripped with myrrh,
my fingers with liquid myrrh,
    on the handles of the bolt.
I opened to my beloved,
    but my beloved had turned and gone.
My soul failed me when he spoke.
I sought him, but found him not;
    I called him, but he gave no answer. (5:2–6)

In her deep yearning, she sets out to find him in vain, and resorts to soliciting her friends' help, imploring them to find him quickly and tell him "I am sick with love" (5:8).

Although the man clearly longs for his woman and finds deep delight in their intimacy, his ardor is never so dramatically depicted. This is important to note. The Bible fully celebrates women's sexual desires and commands husbands to take seriously learning the sweet labor of satisfying their wives.

Further, because this woman knows the power and depth of her sexual longing, three times she implores other women, "I adjure you, O daughters of Jerusalem, that you not stir up or awaken love until it pleases" (8:4; see also 2:7; 3:5). You don't want to heat the oven and fill your home with the savory aroma of a roast and potatoes when you're on a fast! In the same way, the woman encourages her sisters to allow their sexuality to lie dormant until such a time that their deep longings can be righteously satisfied. *This* is the message that the young women participating in abstinence programs need to hear! This is not a denial of the goodness of sexuality but an acknowledgment of its power. It is this intensity of desire that leads Paul to exhort Christians, "But if they cannot exercise self-control, they should marry. For it is better to marry than to burn with passion" (1 Corinthians 7:9). Our sexual yearning is more than a desire for physical pleasure. We long to be one flesh with another because we were created for union with Jesus. That's the true power behind the profound mystery of our sexuality.

CHAPTER 5

Sex in Relationship

Because we are physical beings, physical attraction matters. We naturally respond to certain sights, sounds, and even smells. All of this is in view when God declares his world "very good" (Genesis 1:31). But unlike the rest of the animal world, human sexuality is about more than intriguing pheromones or exquisite plumage. This is particularly evident as the man and woman marvel at one another in the Song of Solomon. It is important to note that the man and woman are delighted with the entirety of the other. In the various passages describing their bodies, both the man and woman praise each other from literally the crown of their heads to their feet. Their delight is in the whole person, not just the sexual parts.

This is very different than the focus of pornography. Porn reduces the individual to sexual body parts—and then zooms in to make these larger than life. While the Song of Solomon praises the sensual delights of sexuality, it celebrates and affirms, rather than reducing, the personhood of both individuals. For example, the man and woman both rejoice in each other's eyes, and they want to look each other in the eye. The man refers to the woman's eyes repeatedly (Song of Solomon 1:15; 4:1, 9; 6:5; 7:4), far more than he describes the explicitly sexual parts of her body. He declares, "You have captivated my heart with one glance of your eyes" (4:9). After a single look he was in that intoxicated state, enchanted. And he pleads, "Turn away your eyes from me, for they overwhelm me" (6:5). When he looks her in the eye, he's consumed with desire.

Consider this focus on her eyes alongside Jesus's teaching: "The eye is the lamp of the body. So, if your eye is healthy, your whole body will be full of light, but if your eye is bad, your whole body will be full of darkness. If then the light in you is darkness, how great is the darkness!" (Matthew 6:22–23). These verses, coming on the heels of Jesus's declaration, "For where your treasure is, there your heart will be also" (v. 21), have led some to make a link between the eyes and heart.[1] This echoes the popular idiom that "the eyes are the window of the soul." Holding these ideas together, there is a sense that when the man is captivated and overwhelmed by the woman's eyes, he is seeing the essence of her as a person. Although there is a physical component to image-bearing sexuality, it is always more than that. For those made in the image of God, sexuality is about union of body and spirit with another. It is always about the wholeness of the individual.

Sex and Union

In his excellent essay, "Sex, Economy, Freedom, and Community," Wendell Berry described the exploitation of sexuality and the consequent diminishing personhood. Commenting on a lotion advertisement depicting a naked, headless woman, he lamented,

> The headlessness of this lotionable lady suggests also another telling indication of the devaluation of sexual love in modern times—that is, the gravitation of attention from the countenance, especially the eyes, to the specifically sexual anatomy. The difference, of course, is that the countenance is both physical and spiritual. There is much testimony to this in the poetic tradition

and elsewhere. Looking into one another's eyes, lovers recognize their encounter as a meeting not merely of two bodies but of two living souls. In one another's eyes, moreover, they see themselves reflected not narcissistically but as singular beings, separate and small, far inferior to the creature that they together make.[2]

As we have seen, there is a "reunion" of God's image-bearers when a husband and wife become "one flesh" in their sexual union. As Berry commented, this new organism represents more than the sum total of the individual parts. The significance of becoming one flesh is evident in a particularly important exchange in the Gospels. Centuries after the giving of the Law, Jesus is challenged about the proper grounds for divorce. Refuting the suggestion that a marriage might be ended for any cause, Jesus pointed to God's design: "Have you not read that he who created them from the beginning made them male and female, and said, 'Therefore a man shall leave his father and his mother and hold fast to his wife, and the two shall become one flesh'? So they are no longer two but one flesh. What therefore God has joined together, let not man separate" (Matthew 19:4–6; also see Mark 10:2–12). Jesus affirms God's created intent remains unchanged, despite the sexual craziness since the fall into sin. Something profound happens at marriage: "They are no longer two but one flesh." God unites disparate but complementary individuals to create a new organism. This is the reason it is not to be put asunder: God has made a "new creation" when he brings a man and woman together in marriage. We must keep this incredibly high view of marriage in mind whenever we consider the biblical prohibitions.

One of the most important passages discussing sexual immorality in the New Testament makes clear that sex is fundamentally designed to unite two human beings physically and spiritually:

"All things are lawful for me," but not all things are helpful. "All things are lawful for me," but I will not be dominated by anything. "Food is meant for the stomach and the stomach for food"—and God will destroy both one and the other. The body is not meant for sexual immorality, but for the Lord, and the Lord for the body. And God raised the Lord and will also raise us up by his power. Do you not know that your bodies are members of Christ? Shall I then take the members of Christ and make them members of a prostitute? Never! Or do you not know that he who is joined to a prostitute becomes one body with her? For, as it is written, "The two will become one flesh." But he who is joined to the Lord becomes one spirit with him. Flee from sexual immorality. Every other sin a person commits is outside the body, but the sexually immoral person sins against his own body. Or do you not know that your body is a temple of the Holy Spirit within you, whom you have from God? You are not your own, for you were bought with a price. So glorify God in your body. (1 Corinthians 6:12–20)

We've already considered how this passage affirms the goodness of our physicality because our bodies are "for the Lord." Just as a husband and wife are united together and so belong to each other, believers are united to the Lord and their bodies are corporately joined to Christ. This union of body and spirit is integral not simply in human relationships but in the fundamental relationship at the core of the Christian life. We are so "one" with God that his Spirit indwells us. He is literally *in* you. In this way, the act of sexual union reflects a profound spiritual reality. The same Spirit responsible for Mary's conception of Jesus (see Matthew 1:20; Luke 1:35) enters us, uniting us with Christ. The primary reason given for *not* engaging in sexual immorality is that our bodies are now the dwelling place of God's Spirit, and God has something better for us, namely himself. Whoever engages in sexual immorality therefore does not simply violate a moral code but damages the "temple" in which the Spirit lives to unite us with Christ. Sexual sin thus wreaks *personal* damage in a way unlike other sins.

This is not to say that sexual sin is worse than other sins. Rather, Paul is telling us that sexuality is a sweet and powerful gift from God, one that is so rich with theological significance, that when it is squandered and abused, we rob ourselves of untold blessings and do violence to our experience of life in Christ. Simply put, sexual sin violates the fundamental reflection of the most glorious union—our connection to our Lord through his Spirit—which is implicit in God's good design of marital love. That's why God cares so much about sexuality and why sexual sin is so profoundly damaging.

While we recognize the severity of sexual sin, it is important to likewise admit that it is universal. Treating sexual sin as particularly terrible drives brothers and sisters dealing with these issues farther underground into shame and isolation. But the truth is that all of us have a fallen sexuality—and actual sexual sins—which need redemption. Since this is so and since "Christ Jesus came into the world to save sinners" (1 Timothy 1:15), we should never treat sexual sin as if it's the sort of thing that only really awful people do. Those who sin sexually share, sadly, in the common state of fallen human life. But they also share the blessed lot of those sinners whom Jesus was rightly accused of befriending (Luke 7:34). We shouldn't see the Bible's severe warnings against sexual sin as distinguishing the "bad" from the "good" among broken humanity, but rather they underscore the incredible theological importance of human sexuality, which makes sexual sin such a big deal. It is because sexuality is so glorious, not that sexual sinners are so despicable, that sex requires such care.

Consider this principle from C. S. Lewis. In arguing for the existence of the devil, he wrote, "The better stuff a creature is made of—the cleverer and stronger and freer it is—then the better it will be if it goes right, but also the worse it will be if it goes wrong." He went on to explain, "A cow cannot be very good or very bad; a dog can be both better and worse" and then extrapolated further that the "better or worse" quality intensifies as you consider a child, ordinary man, genius, and finally "a superhuman spirit" which will be the "best— or worst—of all."[3] This principle applies to our sexuality. God has given us an incredible gift that communicates rich truths about our relationship with him. Sexual sin is against one's own body not because misused sexuality is so horrific in its corruption but because sex is a glorious gift given to humanity and its misuse is a tragic loss to the one who tramples it. The primary reason to safeguard your sexuality is to preserve the sweetness and power of your union with Christ.

Along these lines, Scripture teaches that our sexuality is important because it reflects our union with Christ by his Spirit:

> This is the will of God, your sanctification: that you abstain from sexual immorality; that each one of you know how to control his own body in holiness and honor, not in the passion of lust like the Gentiles who do not know God; that no one transgress and wrong his brother in this matter, because the Lord is an avenger in all these things, as we told you beforehand and solemnly warned you. For God has not called us for impurity, but in holiness. Therefore whoever disregards this, disregards not man but God, who gives his Holy Spirit to you. (1 Thessalonians 4:3–8)

Paul warns against sexual immorality because God "gives his Holy Spirit to you." It's as if God says, "Don't be united immorally to another—I want to be united to you!" The Spirit is the One who binds us into the ultimate union with the Father and the Son. As we consider this passage in connection with those discussed above, I hope you can hear God saying, "I want to fill you. I want to satisfy you. I want to be united to you." His desire for us is so great that he wants to feel what we feel, even groaning with us in our pain. Passages often viewed as only prohibitive of inappropriate sex actually contain a glorious invitation to view sex as holy and honorable. They highlight the greatest mystery behind marital sexuality—Jesus and his longing to be united to his bride.

If you are anything like me, you may hear only condemnation in passages like these. In my fear and doubt, I could read this and think, *If my sanctification is tied to who I am sexually, maybe I'm not even a Christian!* But we tend to put a period where God puts a comma. The last word in this passage is not "therefore whoever disregards this, disregards not man but God," although we may be tempted to stop reading there. Anytime you put down the Bible feeling condemned, you can be certain that was the work of the enemy, not the Spirit. When you are convicted by the Spirit of God in the reading of his Word, you are pointed to Jesus and the hope of the gospel. If you walk away feeling condemned when there is "no condemnation for those who are in Christ Jesus" (Romans 8:1), this is not the work of the Holy Spirit. Through what you read, the Spirit may very well convict you of things that aren't right in your life, but the Spirit woos us to Christ and reminds of his mercy. Don't walk away from the Bible feeling condemned—talk to God! If there is conviction, seek forgiveness and fresh grace to obey. And ask for the Spirit to give you greater strength to hold fast to his promises.

Boundaries and Blessing

You may be wondering, if the Bible is so positive about sexuality, why has the church's teaching seemed so negative?

While the Bible celebrates sex as a good gift of God, it is written in the context of a fallen world. That means the Bible truthfully records some sexually bizarre historical events. It also means there's a lot of space dedicated to reining in sexual behavior. This is particularly true in the New Testament, since so much of it was written to pagan converts with a history of an anything-goes sexuality. But all these warnings against immorality demonstrate that sex is a precious gift to be held in honor.

The early chapters of Proverbs repeatedly warn young men against allowing their sexual desires to run rampant. What is God saying? "These desires are strong by design, but only through following my intention will you experience pleasure that truly satisfies your soul." The power of our sexuality and the reason why the Bible is careful to clearly lay out its constraints reflects its *goodness*.

The world looks at this and sees Christianity denigrating sexuality, but the opposite is actually true: because it is such a glorious good, we guard and protect sex. If a married woman goes for a swim in a public pool, she does not leave her engagement ring sitting poolside, on top of her towel. It is valuable and precious! And not just because of its market value. The ring itself is costly, but it is all the more so because of the relationship it symbolizes. This is a glimpse of the enormous value God places on marital sexuality. The tragedy is to pursue this incredible gift as an end in itself. Imbued with power due to the glories it symbolizes, sexuality wields the potential for amazing blessing, but also unimaginable devastation. We see the brokenness all around us.

This is why Proverbs contrasts the intoxicated delight of marital sexuality with the destruction resulting from indulging wayward desires. Describing a young man going home with a woman to commit adultery, the passage concludes, "All at once he follows her, as an ox goes to the slaughter, or as a stag is caught fast till an arrow pierces its liver; as a bird rushes into a snare; he does not know that it will cost him his life" (Proverbs 7:22–23). Because sex points us to God, it is powerful. Used rightly, it leads to wonderful blessings and deeper worship. Abused, it enslaves and destroys. The unbelievable potency of sex remains, but it becomes a hurricane force of destruction rather than blessing. God's restraint on sexual expression constrains evil but also channels his blessing.

Sexual immorality is thus a form of *folly*. Hebrews 12 teaches, "See to it . . . that no one is sexually immoral or unholy like Esau, who sold his birthright for a single meal. For you know that afterward, when he desired to inherit the blessing, he was rejected, for he found no chance to repent, though he sought it with tears" (vv. 15–17). Why is Esau used to illustrate the importance of sexual purity? The writer employs an important story from Israel's past to indicate the foolishness of distorting the holy gift of sexuality. Jacob and Esau were twins born to Isaac. Esau was the firstborn, and therefore the heir to the lion's share of the family wealth, his birthright. He came home one day exhausted and famished after a day of hunting. Jacob, who preferred to stay home and cook, had a lentil stew simmering over a fire. When Esau asked for some, Jacob offered to trade him his birthright for a bowl of stew. Esau, in what becomes one of the Bible's chief examples of folly, takes the deal. The passage says, "Thus Esau despised his birthright" (Genesis 25:34). Esau took something of incredible value and traded it away for next to nothing—a bowl of thin bean soup. Though even if he was offered a porterhouse steak with all the trimmings, it still would have been a ridiculous deal. The writer of Hebrews is saying that your sexuality, like Esau's birthright, is a wonderful gift of God for you to treasure and steward. Do not trade it away for the cheap satisfaction of momentary cravings. Instead we should treasure and honor our sexuality.

Destined to Bond

Proverbs declares the mystery of romantic love, "Three things
are too wonderful for me; four I do not understand: the way of
an eagle in the sky, the way of a serpent on a rock, the way of
a ship on the high seas, and the way of a man with a virgin"
(Proverbs 30:18–19). Can you feel the sense of awe? The pinnacle of created wonders—which the first three marvels build
up to—is how God created the dance of romantic delight
between a man and woman. There is mystery in the laws of
attraction (why do we tend to pursue someone so different?),
but it is clear that God has intricately formed us to bond in the
marital relationship.

The wonder of sexuality deepening union is affirmed by
science. Modern science is ever-increasing in its knowledge of
the world, and its findings showcase the glory of our Creator.
Scientists have discovered ways that sexual pleasure physiologically strengthens the emotional connection between partners.
Our bodies are the splendid interweaving of the physical and
the spiritual. God's design of our physiology should generate
deep awe and worship. Neurologists have long known that
oxytocin is released through orgasm, breastfeeding, and other
forms of physical contact, causing it to be dubbed the "love
hormone." Chemically, part of the pleasure of an orgasm is the
rush of this hormone flooding your system.[4]

Consider how this chemical phenomenon dovetails with
God's design of monogamy in marriage. Especially if couples
are committed to abstaining from solo sex, the only means
of receiving this pleasure is through one another. The release
of oxytocin is thus intended by God as a means of "chemically bonding" spouses. If we are obedient to his design, this
particular pleasure is dynamically connected to one's spouse
alone. Personally, my wife—and no one else on the planet—
enables me to experience this wondrous pleasure. God created

the release of hormones as part of our integrated physical and spiritual beings to uniquely bond us to another in the covenant of marriage.

CHAPTER 6

Sex Is about Serving Each Other

A number of years ago I sat in a diner talking with a man in his fifties. Married almost thirty years, he lamented the lack of satisfaction experienced in his sexual relationship with his wife. Both of them had been raised in the church and were appropriately inexperienced prior to marriage. My friend was discouraged by the absence of a deeper connection with his wife, and his sense that she was apathetic and disengaged during their physical intimacy. As our dinner progressed, he grew increasingly animated discussing his frustration. He finally flung out his arms in exasperation, exclaiming, "I knew parts of marriage would be hard, but sex was supposed to be easy!" (There were a number of raised eyebrows from the surrounding tables.)

Where did he learn this? Given his Christian upbringing, was this one of the subtle lies resulting from the church's silence? Had he been led to believe that waiting until marriage meant everything would just click? Christian abstinence programs communicate that if only you hold out for marriage, your honeymoon will be *awesome*. Not true, kids; they're lying to you. This message reflects how much these programs have unwittingly bought into the lies of the world about sex and attempt to baptize them for the next generation. What's the message? Sex is best when you are young and hot, surging with hormonal craving. The culture says sex is the ultimate experience; just go for it. The abstinence message only slightly tweaks the imperative: wait till you get married. But the heart of the messages is the same, that sex is about your pleasure. This is the stuff of pop culture, urging our kids not to squander their youth but enjoy the best sex while they still can. Meanwhile, God intends physical intimacy in marriage to grow and mature like every other aspect of the relationship.

The maxim that practice make perfect is true for almost every area of life. Football teams endlessly drill so their plays run like clockwork. The novel that transports you to another time or world makes writing look easy. (It's not. It's really, *really* hard.) The violinist who seems to conjure the notes magically has rehearsed for decades. The seeming ease of these artistic expressions masks the arduous labors behind them. Think about your own career or a hobby you enjoy. Almost any worthwhile endeavor takes a whole lot of practice, trial, and error. The same is true for good sex in marriage. It is the fruit of a lifetime's hard work of deepening emotional and spiritual oneness while being willing to discuss physical intimacy without shame. And, quite practically, it requires lots and lots of practice.

In our present cultural moment, the idea that marriage and sex get better with time is hard to believe. Many of us are the product of broken homes, and the majority of millennials haven't seen a healthy marriage firsthand. Emotional connection, godly conflict resolution, and joyful friendship in marriage are foreign concepts. On the other hand, we are inundated with alternatives to biblical sexuality unlike any previous generation—from internet porn to the hookup culture to acceptance of all things LGBTQ+.[1] In such a world, it is not surprising that we need to relearn what creates wisdom and wholeness in marriage and sex. Like every other aspect of marriage, a mutually fulfilling sexual relationship takes time and effort. Couples need to be intentional to grow in this area of their relationship. Godly sex requires more than just being in God's covenantal context for sexual expression. God planned not just the context but also *how* married people should comport themselves sexually. Your behavior toward each other matters as much as the appropriate context.

Context and Actions

I have worked with many Christian couples who didn't understand that God cares about both the relational context *and* spouses' actions toward each other. Many have the perspective that anything goes sexually in Christian marriage because it is the right relationship for physical intimacy. Some of this is the result of a misinterpretation of Hebrews 13:4. The King James Version's rendering is particularly problematic, "Marriage is honourable in all, *and the bed undefiled*" (emphasis added). This wording leads to the assumption that the marriage covenant whitewashes every sexual behavior, so the marriage bed is de facto "undefiled" because God approves of any sexual behavior in this context. This has been misapplied to teach that once the promises are made, sex is a free-for-all.

The English Standard Version's rendering is much more helpful: "Let marriage be held in honor among all, and let the marriage bed be undefiled, for God will judge the sexually immoral and adulterous." The sentence structure of the Greek "implies the missing third person imperative,"[2] thus it should not be translated "is" but rather "Let . . . be . . ." A more wooden translation of the Greek would read, "Honored let marriage be and let the bed be undefiled." The point is that marriage itself does not make the bed undefiled—the couple needs intentionality to keep their intimacy pure. And this command for marriage to be honored "among all" means that applies to both married and single believers. All of us are called to have a high view of marriage, and the purity of a couple's sexual relationship is a matter of concern for the whole community of faith.

Years ago, I counseled a couple struggling in their marriage. The wife recounted through tears the humiliating behaviors demanded by her husband because he was "the head of his wife," and he said she was called to submit. As a "KJV only" guy, he interpreted Hebrews 13:4 to mean there were no limits to what he could sexually demand from his wife. She was treated like an object daily, subject to his insatiable and increasingly depraved desires. Sadly, their church offered little assistance to the wife's complaints, and because the husband was the pastor's protégé, his wife was painted as hormonal and hyperbolic to the church leadership. This terrible situation is, tragically, not uncommon.

A word to church leaders: if a wife musters up the courage to describe the shame and degradation she feels over what happens in their marriage bed, *believe* her and take those claims seriously! It is incredibly difficult for people to open up about these struggles, especially to male leadership. Just as Jesus welcomed the oppressed and marginalized, pastors should be working hard to communicate their understanding that couples need help in this area of life and that wives may be oppressed by their husbands' abusive behavior (sexual or otherwise). Pastors today have an urgent calling to advocate for and defend women who have been secretly dehumanized in their marriages. At this point, it is important to mention that nonconsensual sex happens in marriage; there is such a thing as marital rape. Given the deep shame and culture of fear that occurs in such marriages, church leaders must regularly communicate that they are aware that marital abuse is a reality and they are present to offer advocacy and protection. This is also an urgent call for churches to take seriously the injunction from Titus 2:3–4 to identify wise, older women who can come alongside young women as role models, sages, and confidants, particularly (but not exclusively) in the realm of marriage.

The Hebrews passage we've been considering identifies two categories of sin that must be avoided to preserve the sanctity of marriage—adultery and sexual immorality. These two categories broadly cover any third-party intrusions, as well as other behaviors that would be considered impure or unchaste. This Greek word *porneia*, translated sexual immorality, has in view not just illicit sexual intercourse but any type of unchastity.[3] Further, the statement that the marriage bed must be "undefiled" is important for at least two reasons. It indicates that, in addition to adultery, there are other practices that defile the marriage bed. Of course, the positive side of this warning describes the "profound mystery" that marriage is *holy*, the opposite of defiled. As mentioned previously, this language is frequently employed in contexts dealing with the priesthood and regulations for worship in the temple. This warning thus depends upon the consistent biblical conviction that the marriage bed is sacred ground, a place that must remain undefiled, since here God meets with and reveals himself to his people.[4]

The Only How-To Passage

Before we consider ways to safeguard against defilement in chapter 7, let's examine godly sexual practice. Although there has been a flurry of Christian how-to books on sexuality in recent years, the Bible is actually pretty silent when it comes to prescribing (or proscribing) specific sexual practices in marriage. But there are big-picture, overarching principles to help us navigate this terrain. In every sphere of life, God provides clear guardrails to steer our behavior in ways that honor him. When it comes to sex in marriage, the most significant passage for consideration is 1 Corinthians 7:1–5:

> Now concerning the matters about which you wrote: "It is good for a man not to have sexual relations with a woman." But because of the temptation to sexual

immorality, each man should have his own wife and each woman her own husband. The husband should give to his wife her conjugal rights, and likewise the wife to her husband. For the wife does not have authority over her own body, but the husband does. Likewise the husband does not have authority over his own body, but the wife does. Do not deprive one another, except perhaps by agreement for a limited time, that you may devote yourselves to prayer; but then come together again, so that Satan may not tempt you because of your lack of self-control.

Many scholars understand the statement, "It is good for a man not to have sexual relations with a woman," as a quote from a letter previously written to Paul by the Corinthian church.[5] As you know, one strand of Greco-Roman philosophy despised the physical world and indulging physical appetites. Our sexual desires' powerful drive was seen as extremely threatening and something that required restraint. After all, if you can achieve self-control in this area, you can rein in anything! In connection with this philosophical view, there may have been a tendency among some of the especially pious Christians in Corinth to abandon marriage and sexuality. Corinth was home to the temple of Aphrodite, the Greek goddess of love. This meant the city contained thousands of prostitutes, a culturally sanctioned institution that was central to the worship of pagan deities. In many respects, first-century Greco-Roman culture still makes twenty-first-century America look pretty tame. In 1 Corinthians, Paul addresses pagan converts to Christianity, some of whom had substantially broken sexual lives (see 1 Corinthians 5:1). It's not surprising that their previous sexual sin, coupled with the unbridled promiscuity of Corinth, led some of these new Christians to look disparagingly at sex and think that maybe the philosophers had a valid point here.

We often view God as holding the huge Book of the Law, the great killjoy in the sky, characterized only by dos and don'ts. Instead of seeing his commands as an invitation to a flourishing life that wisely enjoys relationship with him and his created goodness, we tend to impose excessive restrictions, often as a reaction against idolatrous abuses of creation. I can relate to this. When I came to faith in my midtwenties, I reverted to my fundamentalist past and began to purge. All my secular music had to go, and I swore off movies and television. Given my promiscuous past, I figured I'd had enough sex and should go the "Saint Paul celibacy" route. (Later in this chapter, Paul encourages some Corinthians to forego marriage for the sake of the kingdom; see vv. 25–40.) I am grateful that God placed patient mentors in my life that helped me see things more clearly. But the Corinthians in this passage clearly need some direction.

Paul had visited Corinth and knew it was a hypersexual culture. So, he acknowledges the amount of external and internal temptations and urges the majority of Corinthians to marry because their culture was a constant siren song to immorality. Although he encourages people who are "gifted" with the ability to control themselves to stay single, he knows that sexual desire can be strong, conceding "if they cannot exercise self-control, they should marry. For it is better to marry than to burn with passion" (1 Corinthians 7:6–9). The desire for sexual intimacy is a completely legitimate reason for entering the institution of marriage.

Paul takes the conversation in a doubly countercultural direction. To the sexually immoral, who denied the importance of marriage or its constraints, Paul affirms the exclusivity of the institution, and he encourages God's provision of marriage as a means of satisfying sexual desire by being joined to a spouse of the opposite sex. For those who impugn marriage and denigrate all sexual expression, Paul extols the gift of sex and its importance in marriage. In fact, Paul says that marital sexuality is so important that not expressing love in this way is depriving one's spouse. Sexual intimacy is not an option for married couples—it is a mandate.

Sex Is a Mandate, but . . .

This passage teaches that sexual activity is *commanded* in the call to give "conjugal rights" and the warning not to "deprive one another" (vv. 3, 7). Sex should be a nonnegotiable part of every Christian marriage. (Don't fret—I'll qualify this momentarily!) A more literal translation of the Greek phrase calling spouses to give "conjugal rights" to one another would be along the lines of "repay the debt of affection owed" to your spouse. Sexual activity is intended to be an overflowing expression of the delight a husband and wife have for each other. Sexual pleasuring in marriage is a wonderful obligation that spouses are blessed to repay each other. Scripture anticipates there will be affection, enthusiasm, and delight in your spouse. This ties back to sex as an expression of *yada*, to know. As your spousal relationship grows over the years, the blessings of your sexual intimacy should increase. God anticipates you will have a deepening understanding of why he chose to make *this* creature for you. He intends a growing enthusiasm as you see your spouse as God sees him or her. Against the abstinence program's lie about your awesome honeymoon, in God's economy pleasure and delight grow with time. Think fine, aged wine, not fizzy grape soda!

This is why the passage warns against "depriving" each other. That particular Greek word is used more frequently in economic contexts to describe robbing or defrauding. Beyond the physical yearning, which is hard enough to deny, the lack of sexual intimacy often demonstrates a lack of enthusiastic delight in your spouse. The problem is bigger than unsatisfied sexual desires; a spouse experiences emotional and spiritual suffering when sex is withheld. This point is well illustrated by a pastor's wife who participated in a panel discussion during a woman's breakout session at a church leadership conference. The panel was asked, "What is one thing you have learned that encourages your husband the most?" Immediately she knew the answer, though she needed courage to blurt it out: "Make love to him!"[6] And I think the reciprocal is true as well. Occasionally some wives may be less focused on the pleasure component of sex, but they still want to be delighted in and desired and have that enthusiasm expressed. For their husbands, that might mean intentional romantic pursuit: planning date nights, bringing home flowers, asking about her day and *really* listening, instead of concentrating primarily on sex.

I realize this might be very painful if you are in a hard marriage. Perhaps the lack of physical intimacy leaves you with a constant feeling of rejection in the relationship where you should feel most affirmed. Or there is sexual activity in your marriage, but it feels like a physical act completely disconnected from anything that feels like the "repayment of a debt of affection." Instead of drawing you closer, intimacy shines a bright light on the growing fissure between you. As they age, wives often feel profound rejection, especially if their husbands prioritize porn and self-gratification over *yada*. It is excruciating to be passed over by the one who should affirm and bless you with delight and desire. Similarly, it is painful for husbands to experience rejection if their sexual desires are consistently rebuffed. Men often care a great deal about experiencing the pleasure of sexual release, but they also long for the affirmation of their wives' responding desire. The fact that a sexless marriage is deeply painful for both spouses highlights how important it is for couples to do the work of nurturing this aspect of their relationship.

For those in difficult marriages, I urge you to bring this pain and disappointment to your ultimate Spouse. Talk to the One who loves and delights in you about your feelings of rejection. Let him know the pain you bear in unsatisfied desires.

"Cast all your anxiety on him because he cares for you" (1 Peter 5:7 NIV). Let me urge you to not cop out, saying he already knows. When Jesus taught his disciples to pray, he told them not to ramble on "for your Father knows what you need before you ask him" (Matthew 6:8). But notice the absolutely crucial point: God's sovereignty wasn't a reason not to pray! Jesus continued and taught them the Lord's Prayer. Consider Jesus's healing of blind Bartimaeus (Mark 10:46–52). After ignoring the crowds' rebuke to be silent, Bartimaeus cries out all the louder, and Jesus calls him over. The situation is obvious. Jesus—and everyone else—knows why Bartimaeus is desperate for his attention. But when he stands before him, Jesus asks, "What do you want me to do for you?" Apparently, it is important for Bartimaeus to articulate, "Rabbi, let me recover my sight" (v. 51). In the same way, Jesus invites you to pour out your heart to him.

So, sexual intimacy is commanded for spouses in 1 Corinthians 7 because God carefully set boundaries for *how* sexuality is to be expressed. Sex is mandated, but this passage does not endorse sex on demand! This is an essential corrective to those who misinterpret Hebrews 13:4. To say anything goes in the marriage bed is completely foreign to this text. I have heard horror stories of pastors preaching on this passage and telling wives, "Now go home and have lots of sex with your husband!" There are some problems here. Rather than a lopsided calling of one spouse (the wife) to serve the other (the husband), this passage demonstrates that sex in Christian marriage should reflect the broader New Testament ethic: "Do nothing from selfish ambition or conceit, but in humility count others more significant than yourselves" (Philippians 2:3). This also plays into the age-old stereotype that men want sex more than women. Although that may be true in some marriages, it is certainly not for all and never has been. I have encountered more situations in which a wife, rather than her husband, wishes her sex life was different. The growing epidemic of porn use in the American church means many men and women prefer self-gratification in front of a screen over physical intimacy with their spouses. This tragic reality is increasingly common.

With this backdrop of unhelpful challenges to wives, consider Jesus's teaching on authority and discipleship. After James and John's bold request to be exalted in Jesus's kingdom, seated at his right and left, the other disciples are angry. Do you remember his response?

> "You know that those who are considered rulers of the Gentiles lord it over them, and their great ones exercise authority over them. But it shall not be so among you. But whoever would be great among you must be your servant, and whoever would be first among you must be slave of all. For even the Son of Man came not to be served but to serve, and to give his life as a ransom for many." (Mark 10:42–45)

The last verse is sometimes used as a proof text for the atonement. Although it clearly demonstrates Jesus died for our sin, that's not the main point Jesus is making. It is the culmination of Jesus's teaching on what it truly means to be great and to be his disciple. In stark contrast with this teaching, it is tragic that 1 Corinthians 7 is used to bludgeon women by commanding them to have sex in submission to their husbands' self-serving lusts.

This could not be further from how God calls us to live. Jesus makes clear that greatness and leadership is about service. Ephesians 5:25 affirms the same ethic in the context of marriage, specifically challenging the temptation to selfishness among men: "Husbands, love your wives, as Christ loved the church and gave himself up for her." For the Christian, leadership means to be a servant and being the "head" (see Ephesians 5:23) means laying down your life in selfless devotion to another. The goal of our discipleship is to be like Jesus, the servant of all.

Learn to Serve

The world takes God's intent for sexuality and stands it on its head, so that people are prone to think primarily in self-centered terms about sexual compatibility, asking, "Will you be able to satisfy my needs?" But as we have seen, focusing on personal pleasure is exactly the opposite of God's intention. Rather, sexual expression is an opportunity to "repay a debt of affection." Each spouse is called to be focused on the pleasure of the other.

First Corinthians 7 was revolutionary in its original context. Although Christianity is often labeled oppressive by our culture, our faith is actually incredibly affirming and balancing of the sexes. In a culture that was profoundly oppressive to women, this passage taught that a husband's body belongs to his wife and that a wife's sexual satisfaction is as equally important as her husband's. The lives and experiences of women are thus valued on the same plane as those of men. In the male-dominant society of the Greco-Roman and Jewish world, this affirmation of women made Christianity unique.

According to 1 Corinthians 7:1–5, sex teaches husbands and wives the great blessing of serving one another. That's why even though sex is mandated, the passage leaves no room for sex on demand. Each spouse is called to consider the desires of the other and to serve the other. This how-to passage demonstrates that sex should be practiced *selflessly*. The broader Christian ethic, intended to govern all behavior, includes the intimacy of the marriage bed. Husbands and wives are commanded to live out the discipleship ethic of selfless service in their sexual relationship. This means I am called to use my body to serve my spouse. This is extremely important: the passage does not teach, "Dave, Jennifer's body belongs to you!" It says, "Dave, your body belongs to Jennifer. How can you use it to serve her?"

Spouses, consider your husband or wife first! Do not think of yourself. When you enter the marriage bed, let your spouse's pleasure be foremost in your mind. Make satisfying your spouse your greatest aim. Can you see the beauty in this? When each spouse is concerned primarily with satisfying the other, both will be richly blessed with exquisite pleasure in the marriage bed. When both are committed to giving pleasure, both are able to receive with joy. This is "repaying the debt of affection." Selflessly pleasure one another, to the delight of both your souls.

God's intent is for the practice and expression of sexual intimacy in marriage to be part of our discipleship, conforming us to the image of Jesus. Just as the delight of this gift points to the Giver, this practice points to the One who served perfectly and empowers us by his Spirit to love and serve in whatever relationships and circumstances he ordains. In marital sexuality, Jesus reveals another beautiful condescension, wherein God is giving a tangible picture of the blessedness of selfless service.

Spouses must not selfishly *use* one another. The goal is not to make your spouse the object of your lust but to reflect the self-giving, sacrificial love of God. Image-bearing sexuality is an invitation to enter into the trinitarian dance of self-giving, affirming, honoring love that has bound God together as Father, Son, and Spirit forever. The goal is not *your pleasure*—the goal is to pleasure your spouse. Sexual expression should reflect the wonder that physical intimacy is about our trinitarian God and your relationship with him. Of course, the beauty of this design is that we receive great pleasure in serving our spouses, and this experience of giving and receiving perpetuates the passionate delight of the dance.

In this way, sexuality is one picture of the blessing of living Christ's life in this world. Peter Kreeft has a great quote about the call to live life selflessly:

> The highest pleasure always comes in self-forgetfulness. Self always spoils its own pleasure. Pleasure is like light; if you grab at it, you miss it; if you try to bottle it, you get only darkness; if you let it pass, you catch the glory. The self has a built-in, God-imaging design of self-fulfillment by self-forgetfulness, pleasure through unselfishness, ecstasy by *ekstasis*, "standing-outside-the-self." This is not the self-conscious self-sacrifice of the do-gooder but the spontaneous, unconscious generosity of the lover.[7]

Especially during seasons of relational decline in a marriage, lovers need to be reminded of this basic truth. God gave us 1 Corinthians 7:1–5 because spouses need to be taught that selflessness must govern the marriage bed and serving each other is the path to deep joy and fulfillment. This conforms us further to the image of our ultimate Bridegroom.

CHAPTER 7

Guarding the Gift

In chapter 3, we talked about God's theological intent behind uniting a husband or wife with a mysterious *other*. Practically, this dynamic forces us to learn how to serve. It is a challenge to enter a one-flesh physical union with someone whose body is completely foreign. Even if you diligently studied your junior high health textbook and are able to correctly label all the parts of the other person, you still do not inhabit that body and its response to touch is incomprehensible to you. God, in his infinite wisdom, crafted men's and women's bodies differently. On a very practical level, couples need to talk about what feels good and what does not. There are things a man might enjoy that will not work for a woman—and vice versa.

Not surprising, men are less complicated. Even the structure is simple. And there's no shortage of jokes about the difference in levels of desire, frequency, or required time allotted. Our "otherness" requires work and dying to selfish desires. It forces me to get outside myself to serve and bless another. And this may be more true for men in their marriages. Except in the case of physical disability or erectile dysfunction, a man will ejaculate every time he has sex. Sometimes quickly. Because this is true, men face significant temptation to be selfish in marital sexuality, focusing on personal gratification. This temptation is only exacerbated when regular masturbation has been a formative experience before marriage. And, of course, pornography use worsens the situation in all kinds of ways. I do not know if men are more prone than women to general selfishness. Women do often tend to be more nurturing than men (but not always) and that can help them embrace life with an others-focused bent. I can only speak for myself, not all men, but I needed intentional remediation in this area of life. I am not naturally wired to serve my wife and family, let alone anyone else. My years of porn use and promiscuity prior to faith in Christ only intensified the sinful perspective that sex was for *my* pleasure. By God's grace I slowly learned to become more attuned to my wife and her body. I learned greater self-control and my desire increased to make sexual expression an experience of *yada*, rather than mere pleasure. In this way, sex became a microcosm of God's greater work, maturing me to become more Christ-like in all of marriage. Sexuality is an arena where we learn the blessing of serving another who is radically different. In order to successfully navigate this unfamiliar terrain, it is crucial for couples to have open, honest conversations about sex.

Start Talking

In my experience, most couples rarely discuss their sexual relationship. Intimacy just sort of happens . . . or not. First Corinthians 7:1–5 is an encouragement for couples to discuss sex. How do you determine what it means to "repay the debt of affection" to *this* husband or *this* wife? You need to ask! Sexual intimacy is a precious gift to a married couple. Their one-flesh physical union sets them uniquely apart from every other relationship. Spouses' interests, gifts, and careers may be wildly divergent with little common ground, encompassing many other relationships. But the marriage bed is a sacred place reserved for them alone. Here they are known unlike anywhere else. This is the only place they are supposed to be naked and unashamed.

Consider for a moment how crazy it is that couples do not prioritize discussing their intimacy. Sex is a precious gift. Not only is it the means by which children are produced, it is a source of wonderful pleasure. When things are valuable, we exercise great care with them. We work hard to provide the best life for our children because we treasure them. On a more mundane level, we stay on top of home upkeep and maintenance of our cars, because (for most of us) these are our most expensive possessions. It is important to be a good steward of valuables entrusted to you. And we tend to discuss those things. We talk regularly about our children, houses, finances, and family priorities. Because they're important, we discuss them. Why are we so hands off in an area of marriage most people would agree is incredibly important? I think it demonstrates the depth of shame we still need to overcome in this area of life. We should be talking about sex because it is important. It matters. And in a Christian marriage, we are invited to be free from shame.

You will not learn how to "repay the debt of affection" apart from honest conversation. This is not a do-it-yourself project you can look up on YouTube. Not only could that be *really* problematic, it'd be largely irrelevant. A spouse becomes one flesh with a specific individual. And that person has a unique body and desires. Unless you talk about your bodies, what feels good and what doesn't, which behaviors are exciting and which are awkward, uncomfortable, or even painful, your spouse will have no idea. This means there needs to be conversation before, during, and after intimacy. This is certainly true at the outset of marriage, but the conversation needs to be ongoing. Various life stages present different opportunities and challenges. Over the course of marriage, a couple's sexual relationship will change. In some ways (hopefully!) it will mature and deepen. But if the Lord provides children, they will impact your sex life. And each of their developmental stages will affect your sexual relationship differently. Then add the physical changes in both male and female bodies over the decades as you age. There will probably never be a time in your marriage when you will not need to talk about your sexual relationship.

Despite the importance of communication, sometimes it's not enough, and outside help is necessary. For example, if a spouse is overcoming the impact of sexual abuse, he or she most likely needs the assistance of a therapist with abuse and trauma care experience. Men dealing with erectile dysfunction and women experiencing ongoing pain during intercourse may require medical assistance. Perpetual sexual sin, like porn use, requires godly confrontation and persistent pastoral care. Depending on its duration and severity, it may require more aggressive spiritual intervention. For some couples, there is too much shame, embarrassment, or entrenched behaviors and disappointment. Christian sex manuals can be helpful. In some cases, a Christian counselor would be necessary. Ensure that any therapeutic approach or book has a high view of Scripture and a biblical sexual ethic—this is the biggest concern. For example, many sex therapists heavily promote "educational" pornography videos. Turning to unholy means will not be a path to God's blessing of the marriage bed. As we seek to improve our sexual relationship, we need to keep in view the call: "let the marriage bed be undefiled."

Above all, it is important to view sex as a window into God's bigger intention for all of us in marriage learning to see, experience, and process the world through the eyes of someone wholly other. In this way, marriage invites us to grow in patience, sensitivity, generosity, and real concern for others; that is, it involves a calling to become the person God created us to be.

Sexual Fasting

I mentioned that human sexuality is about more than procreation, not less. If all God cared about was our ability to fill the earth, subdue it, and have dominion, then creating sexes was a bad idea. My single readers may be shocked to hear this, but after a couple years or sometimes even months, and certainly after babies come along or in the profound grief over their absence, the frequency of sexual activity between married couples drops off pretty dramatically. Dealing with exhaustion, a new pace of life, juggling so many responsibilities, while trying to attune the emotional connectivity between you and your spouse, concurrent with the simultaneous physical stirrings requisite for the desired activity . . . Well, you get the point. Sadly, during some seasons, it can seem like the planets need to align for a couple to find time to be intimate.

However, the only reason given by 1 Corinthians 7 for not fulfilling the mandated affectionate debt repayment is "except perhaps by agreement for a limited time, that you may devote yourselves to prayer" (v. 5). Notice that there must be an agreement. The passage anticipates that couples will talk about their sex life. So, there must be an agreement between the couple and a clear time parameter established. It is unusual for a couple to choose this as an intentional area of spiritual fasting. Sadly, I suspect the reasons for a faltering sexual relationship for many couples have nothing to do with spiritual discipline but is the result of other factors in their marriage or life. Because of the clear command to not "deprive" each other, the passage calls for a couple to agree together to forego sex for a set time. It could be helpful for a time of spiritual renewal or perhaps because of urgent concern over a specific issue. I could imagine the news from a prodigal child who's plunged into some deep place of darkness leads a heartbroken couple to fast for a season of intercession for their child. This would likely include periods of fasting from food or entertainment, and perhaps they'd choose to forego sexual intimacy as well. But the passage makes clear there should be consensus and joint intentionality behind this. And it should have a specified time limit.

One word of pastoral concern: if your marriage is sexless (clinically defined as being intimate less than ten times a year), you need to talk with your spouse about this, assuming there aren't obvious physical reasons. Having sex regularly is not necessarily a sign of a healthy marriage, but its complete absence (or extreme infrequency) is a matter of concern if medical issues or advanced age aren't the culprits. It is the largest marital complaint posted online. As we considered briefly, God designed us physiologically to bond through sexual expression and the good feelings produced by the rush of oxytocin. Although there may be imbalances in desire, often both spouses in a sexless marriage are disappointed and frustrated and would like things to be different. So, talk to each other! It may also be helpful to reach out to trusted friends or leaders in your church to help you process the situation as a couple. And the call to pray here is important. If this is an area of challenge in your marriage, Paul warns there is a lot of temptation because sexual restraint takes a lot of self-control. I encourage you to pray individually and with your spouse about this particular area in your marriage.

Is This Okay? Oral Sex as a Case Study

Because God's design for sexual expression is other-focused, there is no room for nonconsensual sexual expression or activity. First Corinthians 7 forbids guilting or manipulating your spouse to do or receive behaviors that he or she may find uncomfortable, shaming, or just gross. There is no room to consider yourself before your spouse—your pleasure, your preferences, your desires—all these things are to be set aside to consider the other. One of the biggest dangers is the way pornography impacts Christian marriage. Porn normalizes behaviors that are deeply subversive and destructive to godly sexual practice. And many young Christian men and women use porn for years prior to getting married. It is naive to assume they are immune to the messages of porn and uninfluenced by the behaviors they've spent hours watching. Tragically, things have spiraled to such a state that even the secular media identifies the negative messages communicated by porn. I read a recent article in *The Atlantic* that challenged the idea, common among young men who use porn, that all women really enjoy anal sex or want to be choked while having intercourse. These are ubiquitous messages of porn that men try to practice on women. The article recounted that some men even attempt these behaviors in the context of a first sexual encounter![1]

My goal is not to exhaustively discuss bedroom behaviors but to give principles to guide a couple's decisions. An issue that's helpful to consider is oral sex. Some have wrongly, I believe, appealed to the Song of Solomon for a biblical warrant for oral sex by conflating evocative metaphor with prescribed practice. At the same time, I do not see a scriptural reason to rule out this practice. The fact that in most cases, it is a "one-way street" regarding pleasure is potentially problematic, but we can put that particular issue to one side for the moment. Considering the discussion from 1 Corinthians 7:1–5 as a grid, oral sex can be a selfless activity. It is a way of serving and blessing another. From that standpoint, there is no particular problem, generally speaking.

But there may be husbands or wives who find either giving or receiving oral sex as unpleasant or worse. If either spouse is uncomfortable, we are now talking about a situation that could violate the call to selflessness. Even though this is not biblically out of bounds *per se*, it is *prohibited* if you coerce or manipulate your spouse to do something he or she does not want to do. Further, in a fallen world, there can be a history of pain and brokenness behind this behavior. A wife whose former boyfriend demanded oral sex may feel cheapened and devalued by her husband's demands. This is only exacerbated by a disappointed husband who wants to experience the pleasure and grows increasingly resentful or demanding. A couple in this situation needs a lot of work on their relationship outside the bedroom and a lot of healing from past sinful behaviors to cleanse the marriage bed from past defiling.

Similarly, a husband may not care about receiving oral sex, but finds giving it to be an exciting means of foreplay. That's fine, unless his wife thinks it's gross. In other words, the issue isn't just demanding to receive a pleasure—demanding to give a pleasure can also be problematic if it's self-focused. In all these things, communication is key. Couples need to talk about how they're feeling about different sexual activities and why. As in the situation mentioned above, there may be a way to find healing from shame and rest in the security of marriage that would leave this wife in a place to joyfully serve the husband she loves without feeling the guilt and shame of her past. But perhaps not. A wife may never want to receive this form of sex, and a husband needs to accept that and find other ways to excite himself and her during foreplay. Conversely, if a wife finds giving oral sex unpleasant, a husband needs to accept that without demanding, pouting, or otherwise manipulating his wife to do what he wants. In your marriage, God opens the door wide and invites you to enter in to sexual pleasure, but always in a way that serves, blesses, and honors your spouse.

So, thinking more broadly to other sexual behaviors, couples need to ask, "Will my spouse feel loved and cherished through this activity? Will our sexual expression promote a sense of comfort and safety in this vulnerable act of love? Will this enhance my spouse's joy and flourishing?" Sexuality is intended to uniquely bond us together and bring blessing to our lives. Because sex is about selfless service, I can't make demands on my spouse. From this standpoint, some things

may be fine for some couples and not for others. And the only
way to sort through this is by honest conversation and careful
listening.

Now, for many couples there is a disparity between each
individual's level of desire. Is it selfish or self-serving to have sex
that only satisfies one spouse? The quick answer: it depends. If
you're the amorous individual, and your desires aren't fulfilled,
do you punish your spouse? Do you pout and have bad attitudes? What about manipulation to coerce sexual favors, such
as "If we don't have sex, I might be tempted to turn to porn
and masturbation instead . . ."? If your non-amorous spouse
feels used or cheapened, there's a problem. However, in any
otherwise healthy marriage, there is a place for one spouse to
serve the other by giving without the expectation of a return.
This is actually quite in line with 1 Corinthians 7:1–5! In his
helpful book, *Sacred Sex*, Tim Alan Gardner describes different sexual experiences in terms of varying quality restaurants.
Sometimes you eat fast food. On very special occasions you
go to an expensive gourmet restaurant. Most of our meals
will fall somewhere in between. He argues fast food can be
loving but in general your sexual diet should consist of more
holistic time together that is mutually satisfying.[2] That said,
demanding that sex is only legitimate if both spouses are able
to climax and insisting on that robs the non-amorous spouse
of the opportunity to bless the other without placing expectations and demands on him or her.

God's design is for you to have sexual conversations, get
to know each other's bodies, and go deeper emotionally and
spiritually in this area of your marriage. Great sex is not the
result of young couples burning with desire, but it happens as
you grow together. And it takes work. Along these lines, be
wary of falling into easy sexual ruts. For example, oral sex
and manual stimulation can be a helpful aspect of foreplay.
Although there can be a place for these behaviors in your relationship, they can be problematic if they become your default

sexual behavior. I have met couples where the only means for the wife climaxing is through oral sex or husbands and wives who can only climax through self-stimulation. In both of these scenarios, the couples should be working toward a more holistic, relational, joint experience.

Imaging Christ and the Church

One clear boundary to sexual expression is that it must be other-focused. In this way, husbands and wives learn the all-important lesson of the deep, satisfying pleasure of serving. When considering godly sexual practice, another crucial consideration is our overall theme verse for this book, Ephesians 5:32. Since marriage is a profound mystery pointing to Christ and the church, in what ways should our sexual practice mirror this spiritual reality? A "no holds barred" view of intimacy goes too far because we need to see our relationship with Jesus behind every aspect of marriage. A couple should be asking questions such as, Is my sexual relationship with my spouse honoring to Christ and his Word? Am I thankful for the blessing of loving him sexually, acknowledging him as God's good gift to me? Do I seek her pleasure first, and do I communicate in our lovemaking my desire and love for her? Does our intimacy reflect the hope of the gospel and Jesus's relationship with us?

It is not merely the union of one man and one woman for life that makes for godly sexuality. We need to express our sexuality in ways that honor our Creator and point to the glory of our union with Christ. We need to avoid two distortions: on one hand, we can have a distorted view of pleasure, not seeing it as a good gift from God to be enjoyed appropriately. The enemy delights in this! Satan, who originally corrupted desire and leads us into worshiping and idolizing the gifts over the Giver, rejoices in the irony of painting God as a killjoy. Tragically, we are doubly deceived by this lie. But another danger is whitewashing all pleasure as inherently good. There are pleasures God forbids. We are warned against drunkenness, and not just to avoid the pain of a hangover. Drinking to excess, even in the absence of next-day consequences, is forbidden because God calls us to be sober and self-controlled. Why? We are to be ruled by his Spirit and nothing else (Ephesians 5:18). We find joy, strength, and courage through the Spirit's empowering.

It is undeniable that there is pleasure in sin. Hebrews describes Moses as "choosing rather to be mistreated with the people of God than to enjoy the fleeting pleasures of sin. He considered the reproach of Christ greater wealth than the treasures of Egypt, for he was looking to the reward" (Hebrews 11:25–26). It takes *faith* to believe God's promised future and deny ourselves forbidden pleasures in the present world. But the whole of Christian faith is staking our entire earthly existence on the life to come. We live in devotion to the One who promised reward after we die. The answer to both of these extremes is to learn to worship God alone and give him thanks for our pleasures. This is what it means to be truly human.

One way some Christians have responded to the church's silence is to go too far in the pursuit of pleasure—almost seeking to baptize the world's obsession with sex while making sure it's kept within the only allowable sexual relationship. However, the goal of godly sexuality is not simply for couples to have as much heightened excitement and pleasure as possible. In fact, Paul warns "in the last days" some in the visible church will be "lovers of pleasure rather than lovers of God" (2 Timothy 3:1, 4). God created sex and wants us to know pleasure in it that leads to thanksgiving and worship of him as the Giver of good gifts. That's the goal. But if we make our goal to experience the most extreme pleasure possible, we will likely go in ungodly directions.

Just as Jesus delights in us and is filled with a holy longing for the consummation on the last day, Christian couples should see their sexual intimacy as a foretaste. Whenever a church celebrates the Lord's Supper, they are looking back at what Jesus accomplished on the Cross for our redemption, and they're looking forward to the wedding feast of the Lamb. Jesus anticipated this at the Last Supper when he declared, "I tell you I will not drink again of this fruit of the vine until that day when I drink it new with you in my Father's kingdom" (Matthew 26:29; also see Mark 14:25; Luke 22:18). Similarly, when a couple celebrates their union through sexual intimacy, it is a dim reflection that points toward the ultimate union with the eternal Bridegroom in the new heavens and new earth. Just as most churches have an appropriately sober practice of the Lord's Supper because of all it entails, so a couple's sexual relationship should honor the deeper truths behind their one-flesh union. This means certain behaviors just do not fit in a Christian marriage, no matter how exciting or pleasurable.

When Mutual Consent Is Inconsequential

It is easy to see why behaviors that make one spouse feel belittled, shamed, and so on do not belong in the marriage bed. But this does not mean mutual consent is all that matters. The other important boundary is that marital sexuality reflects the "profound mystery" of Christ's relationship to his church. Let me share a few examples that have emerged in my work with Christian couples.

Shockingly, *Fifty Shades of Grey* has made bondage, domination, sadism, and masochism (BDSM) mainstream. A pastor friend went to the dentist after the film opened on Valentine's Day weekend. He was so grateful his mouth was stuffed with the hygienist's hands and tools as she told him about going to see it on opening night with *her mother*. A Christian woman's leader challenged *Fifty Shades of Grey* in a blog and was lambasted by dozens of Christian women, including pastors' wives who talked about how these behaviors revolutionized their sexual relationship. Suppose a Christian couple is really excited to practice bondage and domination? Both are on board with this activity, and no one is being coerced or manipulated. Is it okay? I argue that this is a twisting of God's design and has no place in the marriage bed. Think about this through the lens of how sex should image Jesus's relationship with his bride. Jesus came to set captives free and calls us not to submit again to slavery. Further, he tells rulers to not dominate others, but to live as servants. Wanting to be humiliated or dominated is broken sexuality, as is dominating, controlling, or humiliating another person. BDSM behavior is a mockery of the great truths and hopes of the gospel! It in no way emulates the wonder of Christ and his church.

A significant component of these activities involves fantasy role-play. This is a way for a couple to *not* be who they really are (or should be) as husband and wife. These fantasies are often deeply embedded in pornography use. For many, BDSM behavior is tied to demeaning childhood experiences that have been sexualized. I worked with one man who had completely sexualized the experience of getting spanked after a traumatic childhood of relentless corporal punishment from his angry father. Couples should ask themselves why they would need (or desire) to role-play in order to experience sexual pleasure.

This is true of acting out sexual fantasies in general. Although broadly encouraged by secular marriage therapists, sexual fantasy is a violation of God's design for sex on multiple levels. First, the goal of sexual intimacy is to be *known*. To be utterly, starkly vulnerable before another, naked in the *real world*. To be loved, accepted, and delighted in for who you truly are. Concocting sexual fantasies is at odds with truly being known and embracing the goodness of God's created world in the marriage bed. Through sexual fantasy, you're creating an alternate reality, instead of living joyfully in God's world as the person he created you to be with the spouse he has blessed you with. Fantasy is a refusal to live in

God's world, with all its blessings and challenges. Think about it this way: Jesus embraced the Father's will for his life fully and never railed against it. (Even as he wrestled in the Garden of Gethsemane, there was willing submission.) He trusted the promises and looked with perfect faith for their fulfillment. "For the joy that was set before him," Jesus endured the cross (Hebrews 12:2). He lived in the real world in dependent love on the Father's promises to redeem all things.

Jesus lived joyfully and whole-heartedly in the Father's world, embracing the Father's will for his life as "very good." For Christian couples to entertain a fantasy world in their sexual relationship is problematic on two levels. On the sin side, it's rejecting God's will for your life and opting to create an alternate reality. If we're honest, it's dipping a toe into immorality—trying to experience sex in a way God has forbidden while operating within his given confines. For example, if a couple pretends they're strangers, meeting in a bar for the first time and going through the drama of seduction, it is defiling to the marriage bed. Pantomiming immorality is not God-honoring sexuality and diminishes his design. And that leads to the second problem: to engage in these behaviors is to miss the fundamental point God is so zealous for us to understand and know—a one-flesh union where we are truly naked and unashamed in a way that is not attainable in any other relationship in this world because it anticipates the ultimate union that is coming in the new heavens and new earth.

Consider a final awkward example. Some have advocated for couples to engage in mutual anal penetration (utilizing sex toys) because this will heighten pleasure. But a little *careful* research demonstrates that God didn't design our bodies this way. Although you could make the same statement about oral sex (that the mouth wasn't created for that), I think that'd be misguided for a couple reasons. First, the mouth is used for eating, speaking, breathing, kissing. It is multiuse by God's *design*. The anus isn't. It really just has one purpose. Secondly,

there are no health problems related to oral sex (unless someone previously contracted an STD, because many can be
transmitted orally), but there are from anal sex. You'd be hard-
pressed to find a physician who wouldn't caution you against
this behavior because of the health ramifications. There are
tremendous risks of blood infections, long-term tissue damage,
rupturing the colon, and so on. In fact, researchers surmise the
pronounced uptick in interest in anal sex is the result of porn's
nearly ubiquitous stranglehold on American men as it prolifer-
ates lies, including the lie that anal sex is something women
really enjoy.

There are clear practical reasons why this is not godly
behavior, but these are tied to gospel implications. Human
history is hurtling forward to the coming wedding feast, the
beginning of the new heavens and new earth. The idea of
new creation throughout the Bible anticipates the reversal of
the curse and the restoration of the world to what our Father
always intended it to be, a place of blessed flourishing.[3] Hear
this important distinction: freedom is not the absence of rules
but is living according to our created intent. A goldfish is not
free when it jumps out of the fishbowl, breaking that con-
straint. It is free when it stays in the water, living the way it
was designed. Similarly, in the new heavens and new earth our
bodies will be perfectly consistent with their design. Engaging
in behaviors that are harmful, damaging, or dehumanizing to
our bodies is inconsistent with their design and a reflection of
life under the curse of sin.

There are many other examples we could consider, such
as getting drunk or high to make sex more pleasurable. Other
risky behaviors include auto-asphyxiation for the purpose of
intensifying the experience of orgasm. In addition to other
people, there should not be other nonhuman "intruders" in
the marriage bed, such as porn or any outside stimulation to
make sex more exciting, taking the focus off your spouse. This
may include using sex toys to enhance pleasure. I realize that

in certain unusual circumstances (like one spouse having a disability), there may be some benefit to utilizing sex toys, but in general anything outside the couple should be seen as an intruder in the marriage bed. Using them creates particular danger when devices can create greater pleasure than your spouse can provide.

Husbands and wives should work toward a sexual relationship that exalts the beauty of Jesus's self-sacrificial devotion to his bride. That can happen only when lines of communication about sexual practices are open between the couple. If one person is repeatedly trying to push for behaviors that make the other uncomfortable, it probably warrants reaching out to others to speak into the situation. There is likely a power dynamic askew in the relationship, and this is just one place where it manifests. The bottom line is that more than consent matters.

Practice Makes Perfect

My friend who thought sex in marriage would be easy could not have been more mistaken. *A satisfying sexual relationship is not easy!* But it is worth the effort you put into it. One of my colleagues at Harvest USA just celebrated his forty-sixth wedding anniversary. God has done a beautiful work of sexual redemption in his life, bringing him out of years of bondage to pornography (which occurred while he served as an elder in his church). He describes his sexual relationship with his wife as better than ever before, but he makes clear that what's going on in their bedroom is not like a porn film. They're both in their midsixties. There are no crazy calisthenics. What makes it so great? *It's her.* This amazing woman he has known and grown with over decades. It's the shared history they bring into the bedroom, raising children, and now blessed with grandchildren. This woman really knows him. And despite all the relationships in his life, this is the only one marked by this sweet intimacy. It's not without challenges, but it is a blessing. And he makes clear that now, more than at any other point in their relationship, his focus is completely on her in their intimacy.

I mentioned earlier that at certain seasons, finding time for intimacy can be like aligning the planets. Nevertheless, we must do what it takes to make sex a priority. Do you need to turn off the TV? Put down your smart phone? Learn how to maintain better boundaries around your career? Let me encourage you to build in emotional and spiritual oneness, if it's lacking, so that your physical relationship is a deeper celebration. My wife and I have two teenagers and two preschoolers—I understand the challenges of time and other pressures. But in your relationship, this is one area you will not regret investing in. We've spent many Saturday evenings watching a movie only to agree while the credits roll that it was a waste of time. We've never set apart an evening for intimacy and afterward lamented, "Why did we do *that*?!" Do the hard, sweet work of growing this area of your marriage. It will lead to greater closeness with your spouse, increasing gratitude to God for the gift of your spouse, and deepening worship as you glimpse, as in a mirror darkly, the wonder of the ultimate union fast approaching.

CHAPTER 8

Single Sexuality

Regardless of our marital status, all of us are gendered, sexual beings. Does the Bible have more to say about single sexuality than "Just say no!"? There is no doubt that it is challenging to be single, yet the Bible suggests that for some this is a "gift" (see 1 Corinthians 7:7–9). Although many singles struggle without a spouse and long for marriage, I know others may not resonate with the feelings of loneliness discussed below. Many single Christians live joyful, content, and especially fruitful lives for the kingdom, specifically because of their unmarried state. I know the challenge of singleness later in life. As I mentioned, after twelve years of marriage, I suddenly lost my first wife to complications from breast cancer—her diagnosis to her death was just five weeks. It was really more like a car crash. I was thirty-nine years old (with twin eight-year-old girls). After her death, I was single for almost three years. While my personal experience with singleness is limited, I do write with a keen awareness of the difficulties singles face. While every person's story is different, I hope that in what follows I may be able to offer something helpful to single readers as they seek to faithfully embrace their sexuality.

I have heard people refer to singleness as the gift nobody wants. While a single, during one holiday season I joked with a friend that I really hoped I wouldn't keep finding *that* gift

under the tree each year! Christmastime was especially difficult. Happy couples were holding hands everywhere I turned.
The whole world seemed paired off. Springtime was hard
too—watching the robins perform their mating dance in the
backyard while the squirrels scampered about. I remember
taking my daughters to the park one fine spring morning only
to find hundreds of stink bugs mating all over the playground
in the warm sunlight. I had some frustrated words with God
that day. If you struggle in your singleness, I know you understand these experiences. Family and people at church are
often unhelpful. One single woman in her thirties recounted
the pain of being put at the kids table every holiday gathering, while watching her significantly younger cousins move up
to the adult table after marriage. As so many people remain
single later in life and the percentage of those who will never
marry continues to rise, the church needs to create rich community beyond the standard family-based programs that have
been the staple for decades.

The pain of being single *again* has its own unique challenges, whether this results by death or divorce. Many are
the only parent, forced to fill the shoes of both. And for those
who still have an ex-spouse in the picture, there are additional challenges with co-parenting: drama from remarriage
and blended families and dealing with the fallout of broken-
hearted kids. Exacerbating all this, many in the church are
unaware of these tremendous challenges. While a single
parent, I remember someone sharing they had invited a man
and his kids over because his wife was away for the weekend
and they felt so bad he was home alone. I kept a straight face,
I think, so this person never knew how painful that was to
hear. I longed for people to invite us over. The weekends were
so hard. Single parenting can be an excruciating and incredibly lonely road.

Single and Waiting (on the Lord)

There's a kid's show called *Daniel Tiger's Neighborhood* (a spin-off of the beloved *Mister Rogers' Neighborhood*). The refrain of one of the songs is, "It's very, very, very hard to wait!" Can I get an amen? As discussed in chapter 1, the creation of Adam and Eve suggests that waiting on the Lord was built into the world from the beginning. Because there we see the eventual blessing as Adam meets Eve and erupts in the first recorded rush of emotion in poetic exultation. But waiting is more pronounced and painful after Genesis 3. There is a reason why there are multiple complaints of "How long, O Lord?" in the Psalms. Life in a fallen world is filled with disappointments and unfulfilled dreams. As Proverbs 13:12 expresses, "Hope deferred makes the heart sick, but a desire fulfilled is a tree of life." Many of us are living with the deep heartache of hope deferred. I can remember seasons of life when the new heavens and new earth seemed a tiny pinprick of light at the end of a vast, decades-long, dark tunnel. It seemed I'd be waiting for blessing until I was invited to partake of the real tree of life in the new creation.

If this is your experience, I want to share a perspective on waiting. It is an active place. I used to think waiting meant sitting on my hands, trying to be patient, like waiting for the bus with nothing to do. Not so. Waiting on the Lord is active. In fact, it is a place of warfare. Years ago, reading through the Psalms, I was struck by the conclusion of Psalm 27, "Wait for the LORD; be strong, and let your heart take courage; wait for the LORD!" (v. 14). Do you hear what David is saying? Waiting on the Lord is a terrifying place to be. It requires incredible, Spirit-given strength. It is not for the faint of heart. Courage is not the absence of fear; it is moving forward despite your terror. This idea is captured well in an old movie called *Braveheart*. William Wallace, a thirteenth-century Scottish noblemen, led

the outnumbered Scots in an unlikely victory against the powerful English army. There is a dramatic scene in which the Scottish infantry faced the English cavalry. As the English advance,
hundreds of horses galloped thunderously across an open field
toward the Scots, with the English riders brandishing spears
and battle axes. Wallace had prepared long wooden stakes
to thwart their attack, but the catch was the men had to wait
until the horses were virtually on top them, otherwise the riders
would see the trap and have time to avert course. As the hoofs
pounded ever closer, the men's eyes widened in fear but Wallace
kept calling out, "Hold, hold!" Finally, just before the horses
trampled down the line of quavering men, Wallace shouted the
order and the thicket of spears sprung up, impaling the steeds
and decimating the cavalry.[1]

This is what waiting on the Lord looks like. Waiting is
not passive. It is a terrifying place of warfare. It takes incredible strength and reliance on God. This is true for any waiting
God calls us to, but especially the waiting that stretches on for
years and decades. If you are wrestling with your singleness, I
encourage you to see this as a battle that takes courage and a
place where God wants to meet you.

Kingdom of the Messiah

In the Old Testament, marriage is assumed to be the normative
mode of life, with childbearing as a critical component. This
is partly due to the creation mandate "to be fruitful and multiply" (Genesis 1:28), as well as the building anticipation that a
deliverer would come from Abraham's seed, a son of David, to
free Israel from her foreign oppressors. But the focus on physical generation begins to shift as Isaiah prophesies about this
coming deliverer.

Isaiah 53 is one of the most wondrous passages pointing to
Jesus's sacrificial death. Written hundreds of years before his

earthly life, it describes his crucifixion and even the manner of his burial. After describing Jesus's death and the reality that he was "cut off" from his generation and the land of the living (v. 8), the passage turns and makes a shocking pronouncement: "Yet it was the will of the LORD to crush him; he has put him to grief; when his soul makes an offering for guilt, he shall see his offspring; he shall prolong his days; the will of the LORD shall prosper in his hand" (v. 10). There is an anticipation of life after death—resurrection!—and the production of *offspring*. Although Jesus lived his perfect human life as a single man and was literally childless, Scripture, looking forward not only to Jesus's resurrection but to the re-creation of the entire cosmos, regards Jesus's single life as having produced a *family* in the community of his followers. This is a striking claim in the ancient world, in which married life and the production of physical children was the assumed norm.

Isaiah goes on to describe the drastic change that is coming with the advent of the Messiah:

> Let not the foreigner who has joined himself to the
>   LORD say,
>   "The LORD will surely separate me from his
>   people";
> and let not the eunuch say,
>   "Behold, I am a dry tree."
> For thus says the LORD:
> "To the eunuchs who keep my Sabbaths,
>   who choose the things that please me
>   and hold fast my covenant,
> I will give in my house and within my walls
>   a monument and a name
>   better than sons and daughters;
> I will give them an everlasting name
>   that shall not be cut off." (56:3–5)

This was an incredible statement! The Old Testament law declared that no one with damaged or removed genitalia could even enter God's assembly (Deuteronomy 23:1). Such people were second-class citizens, at least as far as worship in the temple was concerned.[2] In such a context, Isaiah's pronouncement was a strong affirmation that God saw those who, through their physical and relational status, were excluded from a central aspect of Israel's religious life. Isaiah envisions a new day when, in a transformation of the creation mandate, begetting children is no longer the primary means of increasing the people of God. Laying out this history highlights the extraordinary redirection that results from Jesus establishing the kingdom of God. Isaiah thus offers singles something "better than sons and daughters"—an everlasting legacy based solely on the work of God through his people bringing about a spiritual generation that carries into the world to come.

Single for the Kingdom

Approaching the New Testament, this change becomes even more pronounced. When Jesus is questioned about the practice of divorce, he brings his listeners back to God's original intent at creation. But he concludes his teaching about the permanence of marriage with a profound declaration: "Not everyone can receive this saying, but only those to whom it is given. For there are eunuchs who have been so from birth, and there are eunuchs who have been made eunuchs by men, and there are eunuchs who have made themselves eunuchs for the sake of the kingdom of heaven. Let the one who is able to receive this receive it" (Matthew 19:11–12).

Instead of insisting on the importance of marriage and the production of children to fulfill the creation mandate, Jesus proclaims that some people will choose singleness for the sake of God's kingdom. This is the first time in the Bible that singleness is depicted as a *desirable* and even *exalted* state! As we'll see below, this is because of the heightened focus on the kingdom that corresponds with the coming of Christ.

Paul takes Jesus's exhortation even further, encouraging the believers at Corinth to seriously consider lifelong singleness because spouses are divided in their loyalties, wanting to serve the kingdom but also wanting to bless their spouses (1 Corinthians 7:6–9, 25–40). Do you see what he's saying? In view of the radical reorienting call to serve in Jesus's kingdom, Scripture understands that mission is so worthy, it ought to be prioritized above the creational calling to "be fruitful and multiply and fill the earth" (Genesis 1:28). Paul's concern is for believers to maintain "undivided devotion to the Lord" (1 Corinthians 7:35) above everything else. To this end, he encourages lifelong celibacy, although he freely acknowledges that it is not sinful to marry. (Also see Paul's clear refutation in 1 Timothy 4:1–3 of those who forbid marriage.)

I do not know how frequently the 1 Corinthians 7 passage just mentioned is preached in American churches. My hunch is not too often. The American church typically portrays marriage and family as the normative ideal. The goal of a singles ministry is to get everyone paired off and participating in the rest of the life of the church: coming to potlucks with casseroles (instead of a bag of Doritos), producing offspring to populate the children's ministry, and so on. For many churches, children are still their best church-growth strategy. Although churches acknowledge that in Christ things are different than the Old Testament, they still operate as though what matters most is getting married and having children. I was preaching at a church in downtown Philadelphia and met a single guy in his thirties who brought a greeting from a mutual friend who lived out of the area. As we chatted, he shared about his move to the city. Even though he continued to work in the distant suburbs, he opted for a long commute, changing churches and moving into the city because in that context he, as a single man, is not the bizarre anomaly he'd been in his former, suburban church. There has been little affirmation—at least in American suburban churches—of the New Testament's high calling of singleness.

Singles have a unique calling and challenge to embrace Christ as their Bridegroom. Despite the hardships, singles have an invitation to a life of devotion to Jesus and relationship with him that is different than it is for married people. Even though we are delighted in our marriage, my wife and I have both realized that there was an intimacy with Jesus we experienced as singles that we've lost now that we have each other and the routine rigors of family life. I don't say this to exalt the monastic life over the "worldly" state of marriage, but am merely acknowledging the truth of Paul's warning that our interests are divided when we're married. According to the New Testament passages above, singles are not second-class citizens, but should be on the front lines of the church's mission. To this end, the church needs to embrace singles, realizing that their unique position and gifts—lauded by the apostle Paul—are a wonderful asset to the church.

A New One Flesh

Way back in Genesis 2:18 when God declared it was "not good" for Adam to be alone, he created Eve and instituted marriage. How can Jesus and Paul pull off this switcheroo against the previously prescribed remedy for humanity's loneliness? What has changed? *The church.* Singleness is a viable, perhaps even preferable, option because now there is a new-creation antidote for humanity's loneliness. Or to put it another way, we now have access to the true community God intended for his people. Just five chapters later in 1 Corinthians 12:12–31, Paul describes the church as a body with all the parts inextricably linked together. Do you hear the overlap with the "one-flesh" language of Genesis as Paul explains our interconnectedness as Christians? The social and communal reality of the church's common life in Christ is the reason Paul encourages singleness for the sake of kingdom. God's people do not *have* to marry because in the body of Christ there should be no lonely Christian. The church is called to be salt and light, reflecting genuine community in our increasingly fractured society.

As I approached adulthood, I looked desperately for community—a true brotherhood of humanity. I looked in a lot of wrong places. I joined the ragged remnant of the peace-and-love-hippie movement twenty years late in the eighties, which basically meant using drugs and following around the Grateful Dead. (It's true: I wore tie-dyes and had an afro.) Just beneath a thin veneer of kindness, I discovered quite a lot of selfish people using and abusing one another. After a series of mishaps (including mounting addiction, selling drugs, and eventual arrest), I ended up in Narcotics Anonymous. Maybe this was real community? But here I discovered an only slightly less-tarnished version of what I had already experienced. By God's amazing grace, I eventually found my way into the church. Now, admittedly, the church still has a *long* way to go. There are innumerable ways the body is still a mess. But the church *is* the body of Christ—this is crucial—and it's the closest thing I have found to real community that actually works.

There are also important implications here for married people. The fact that a married couple is one flesh should not be understood to mean that any couple is self-sufficient apart from the church. Married people are corporately a single body part in Christ's body and still need the rest of the body. Marriage is an exclusive, covenantal relationship, but it can't be your *only* relationship. As it is not good for any individual to be alone, it is also not healthy for any specific relationship to be alone, in isolation from the wider network of relationships God has designed to shape our lives in the body of Christ. In the broader culture and the church, there is often pressure for spouses to be one another's best friends and soulmates. This often results in diminishing other relationships and can put inordinate pressure on marriages (or potential marriages). Such an approach to marriage is destined for failure, since it puts burdens on spouses they can't possibly bear and ignores the call from Scripture to live in community.[3]

The identity of the church as the body of Christ means that a lonely Christian should be oxymoronic. Scripture promises, "God sets the lonely in families" (Psalm 68:6, NIV). There is a new context in which to be known. But I'm concerned, knowing many lonely, especially older, singles, that we are falling short of our calling. The majority of churches are built around programs that assume marriage and children, so singles fall through the cracks, particularly if they age out of the requisite "singles ministry."

We are living at a time when more people remain unmarried later into life, if they marry at all. While our society becomes increasingly fragmented and disconnected (apart from the superficial gloss of social media which can do more harm than good for folks already feeling isolated and depressed), the church has a wonderful opportunity to be countercultural and embrace everyone into the family. This is particularly true for older singles, especially those wrestling with same-sex attraction. Many of these brothers and sisters will not marry. Do you know the repeated concern I hear from single men in their fifties with same-sex attraction? They say, "I don't want to die alone." They are terrified of battling a terminal disease in isolation or wasting away, abandoned and alone, in a nursing home. Our primary calling as Christians is to love one another. Although this extends beyond the church—even to our enemies!—excelling in loving single brothers and sisters is a great place to start.

What steps need to be taken to enfold singles into their rightful place in the body? Ephesians 4:15–16 tells us that the body only reaches maturity as "each part is working properly." This means if singles are not fully engaged and exercising their gifts, the maturity of the entire body is significantly hindered. In what ways may our churches be anemic and deficient because singles are underutilized and unappreciated? Where does your own church need to grow in this area? There are two equally important aspects to consider: first, making sure there are no lonely people in the body. Second, don't see singles as only lonely, needy people. They are gifted, equipped, and necessary for the health of your church! Married people need singles as much as singles need married people.

Spiritual Progeny

As I have already said, single people have a unique opportunity to serve the kingdom. Instead of focusing on their own nuclear family, single Christians have the opportunity to nurture and disciple far more people. Paul's life is an amazing picture of this, and his correspondence with individual churches demonstrated the depth of his care for them. Rather than being focused on cultivating his own personal happiness, he describes his life as one given to others: "We were gentle among you, like a nursing mother taking care of her own children. So, being affectionately desirous of you, we were ready to share with you not only the gospel of God but also our own selves, because you had become very dear to us" (1 Thessalonians 2:7–8). Interestingly, though single and male, Paul likens his ministry to the love and selflessness of a tender mother. He also described his work in paternal terms: "For you know how, like a father with his children, we exhorted each one of you and encouraged you and charged you to walk in a manner worthy of God, who calls you into his own kingdom and glory" (2:11–12). He concludes this discourse with a focus on his fellow Christians as his *children*: "For what is our hope or joy or crown of boasting before our Lord Jesus at his coming? Is it not you? For you are our glory and joy" (2:19–20). As far as we know, Paul had no biological children, but it is clear from the richness of these descriptions that he lacked nothing relationally, given his deep love for those he served in the church.

He demonstrates the same warmth and love toward the Corinthians, who notoriously made his life and ministry extremely painful. He exclaims, "You yourselves are our letter of recommendation, written on our hearts, to be known and read by all" (2 Corinthians 3:2). Paul feels great agony over the divisions, sexual sin, and legal entanglements he confronts in 1 Corinthians, including the influence of the so-called super-apostles, who challenged his authority and made his ministry difficult. But he writes with the love—and heartache!—of a parent: "I wrote to you out of much affliction and anguish of heart and with many tears, not to cause you pain but to let you know the abundant love that I have for you" (2 Corinthians 2:4; also see Galatians 4:19). I do not need to belabor the point—Paul saw the Christians among whom he planted churches (and even those he'd never met) as his spiritual family. Although deeply pained at times, his spiritual kinship was also his principle source of joy. Holding together Paul's encouragement to remain single for the sake of the kingdom and the evident fruitfulness in his life should be a source of encouragement to singles. Part of Paul's rationale in 1 Corinthians 7 is that singles can be even *more fruitful* in the spiritual ways that ultimately matter most. They are invited to be undivided in their devotion to King Jesus as they labor to extend the boundaries of his kingdom.

In light of this invitation to bear fruit in Christ's kingdom, hear this wonderful promise from Isaiah: "'Sing, O barren one, who did not bear; break forth into singing and cry aloud, you who have not been in labor! For the children of the desolate one will be more than the children of her who is married,' says the LORD" (54:1).

Working through the Pain

I realize for many unmarried Christians this vision may not seem to offer much comfort. I once preached on Malachi 2:10–16. In this section, the ancient tribe of Judah is rebuked for divorcing their wives from among their own people in order to marry foreign women who worship idols. Malachi rages, "Did he not make them one, with a portion of the Spirit in their union? *And what was the one God seeking? Godly offspring.* So guard yourselves in your spirit, and let none of you be faithless to the wife of your youth" (v. 15, emphasis added). As I discussed this passage, I tried to share some of the vision of singleness I have been commending in this chapter—that singles have opportunities to nurture spiritually-generated "offspring." Some single folks in the church were encouraged by this, but others felt it wasn't enough. Many single people—and not only women—want actual physical offspring. They want to be parents. They want to hold their own children. What can we say to such a widespread and understandable human desire? In view of such unique disappointments in the lives of many single people, along with God's special design of marriage at the creation, we may be forced to conclude that singleness, with all its challenges, is one aspect of the brokenness of the world due to the fall. If this is an accurate assessment, it means singleness may always come with an ache on some level. For some it is a "gift," and presumably, they have "self-control" and do not "burn with passion" (1 Corinthians 7:7, 9). But the fact is that many face singleness for a host of reasons while *not* experiencing a sense of having been designed for it.

I suspect, for many singles in twenty-first-century America, singleness is a gift they never wanted but has been thrust upon them. They struggle profoundly with self-control, consumed with flames of passion they can't righteously quench. And it is not just sexual desire. It's everything—the delight of producing children and enjoying a family and having a mate to share life's joys and trials. Not having that can be a real experience of loss, and needs to lead the church not only toward deeper empathy for singles but to a more searching, spiritual apprehension of God's wisdom for us in the face of such trials.[4]

I already mentioned I was single in my forties for a relatively brief period. While this experience has certainly not made me the wisest person on this topic, I do have a few thoughts to share, learned through this season's pain. First, I found it necessary to honestly wrestle with God about my heartache. In Hebrew, the name Israel means "one who wrestles with God." This is what it means to live in a real relationship with God. The Psalms had long been an important part of my devotional life, but they took on even deeper meaning in my grief. Why? They are far more honest than most Christians! And, as a seminary professor once showed me, the Psalms, by virtue of their poetic, existential nature, are uniquely suited to help us articulate our own experiences. At a particularly low point, a brother asked me how I was doing. I replied, "I'm hanging in there." Unfeelingly, he responded with an out-of-touch admonition, "I wish you'd said, 'I'm standing on the Rock!'" It was all I could do to smile and walk away. (The other option was to shove him down the stairs, but the Spirit made it clear that wasn't Christ-like and that a father with an assault and battery conviction wouldn't help my daughters at all.) In contrast to that Christian, the Psalms are painfully honest about life in a fallen world. Over 40 percent of them may be classified as psalms of lament, as they call out to God with tremulous voice because of the pain of life in this world. Scripture does not sugarcoat the truth that life is *hard* and that our experiences often seem to run counter to God's promises. This is why his people have always "wrestled" with him—if they are being honest.

One of the exhortations in 1 Corinthians 7 is "let each person lead the life that the Lord has assigned to him, and to which God has called him" (v. 17). This is where the "wrestling with God" needs to happen. If you are single, this is the life God has assigned to you, at least for now. Consider these passages, which discuss God's mysterious ordering of the things we can't control in our lives:

> Your eyes saw my unformed body; all the days ordained for me were written in your book before one of them came to be. (Psalm 139:16, NIV)

> The heart of man plans his way, but the LORD establishes his steps. (Proverbs 16:9)

> And he made from one man every nation of mankind to live on all the face of the earth, having determined allotted periods and the boundaries of their dwelling place. (Acts 17:26)

If God is truly God, there is no getting around the fact that he is behind everything in existence. His sovereignty is behind your singleness. If you're not happy about it and you're not talking to him, you need to start. Because I guarantee you this—whether you are speaking directly about this issue or not, it affects your relationship with him. Perhaps you are ignoring him in your pain, shutting him out (sadly, this is one of my personal tactics). And, of course, if you're shutting him out, you're turning somewhere else to medicate your pain. Maybe you're losing yourself by searching Christian Mingle, Netflix binging, or trying to assuage your desire with porn or romance novels. Or perhaps it's alcohol, work, exercise, or food. Or a combination—eating ice cream doused in chocolate liqueur, while doing work on your laptop, sitting in front of Netflix on your smart TV, while occasionally swiping through potential dates on your tablet . . . twenty-first-century idolatry can certainly multitask.

As I have already confessed, I struggled with managing my pain when I was single. I hated facing an empty bed, so I put it off until I was so utterly exhausted that I would just collapse. But a profound change started happening when I stopped avoiding and courageously faced the empty bedroom at a reasonable time of night. A regular routine of intentionally engaging God in the quietness of my house, once my daughters were in bed, became a source of new, quiet resilience.

In addition to the Psalms, I found solace in the companionship of other Christians who had suffered. I made connections with brothers and sisters in a Grief Share group and began to gather with a group of men who had faced the same grief, my "Widowers Fraternity." Equally significant was finding writers who (like the Psalms) put words to my pain and pointed to Christ as my hope. The seventeenth-century Scottish theologian, Samuel Rutherford, has probably been my most-valued mentor across the centuries. He wrote out of his own pain and loss. Countering the "standing on the Rock" comment mentioned above, consider this line: "He taketh the [little children] in His arms when they come to a deep water; at least, when they lose ground, and are put to swim, then His hand is under their chin."[5] When I read Rutherford, I knew he understood what it was like to feel completely overwhelmed in a rising flood. But he reminded me that Jesus's hand was under my chin. I might have felt as if at any moment I was about to go under (I would much prefer being borne high above the waves!), but there was always a strong, steady hand under my chin that wouldn't let me drown. Now, a seventeenth-century theologian may hold no appeal for you, but you'll need to find something to help you intentionally draw near to God in the midst of lonely solitude.

The critical thing was that I started intentionally engaging God in my pain. I learned he is the God of all comfort when I learned to lay in bed and weep, pouring out the pain in my heart. I screamed and wailed when my daughters weren't home. (Fortunately, my neighbor on the other side of the wall in my not-quite-soundproof townhouse knew about my life circumstances and never called 911.) I learned that comfort comes on the other side of expressing the pain—choosing not to medicate it but facing it honestly with him. The only way to find your way to peace with this issue is to honestly fight your way through the pain.

Embracing Promises Amid Pain

While the truth of God's sovereignty sometimes sounds cold and distant, I urge you to see it in light of his amazingly particular love for you. David, considering God's close attention to the details of his life, declares, "Such knowledge is too wonderful for me; it is high; I cannot attain it" (Psalm 139:6). He goes on to describe God's thoughts toward him as innumerable as the grains of sand. (Think about that at the beach this summer!) God's thoughts toward you are vast and particular and fine-tuned to your unique life. In the context of this particular love, we should think of his sovereign work that guides the details of our lives.

Consider the amazing declaration of Isaiah: "But now thus says the LORD, he who created you, O Jacob, he who formed you, O Israel: 'Fear not, for I have redeemed you; I have called you by name, you are mine. . . . You are precious in my eyes, and honored, and I love you. . . . everyone who is called by my name, whom I created for my glory, whom I formed and made' " (Isaiah 43:1, 4, 7). Not only did God create and form you to be a unique image-bearer, but he calls you *by name* as his very own. Because you are incredibly precious and loved, his eyes are on you and he wants to honor you. The ultimate Bridegroom does not leave you alone; he gives you his name. And, finally, did you catch why he created you? *For his glory!* Alongside these incredible statements, the New Testament teaches that Jesus "gave himself for us to redeem us from all lawlessness and to purify *for himself a people for his own possession* who are zealous for good works" (Titus 2:14, emphasis added). Do you hear the Bridegroom language? He wants to possess you as his very own, and that's why Jesus came—to win his bride. I love these lines from the great, old hymn "The Church's One Foundation":

> From heav'n He came and sought her
>   To be His holy Bride;
> With His own blood He bought her,
>   And for her life He died.[6]

If you are single, I long for you to hear these words as deeply true, rather than spiritual platitudes. Jesus wants to meet you in your pain, disappointment, and unsatisfied desires, and give you comfort—this is a profound spiritual reality. Jesus promised, "I will not leave you as orphans; I will come to you" (John 14:18). He knows our deep need for him, and he longs to be intimately united to us.

The Holy Spirit is the gift of Jesus's presence with us— "the guarantee of our inheritance until we acquire possession of it" (Ephesians 1:14). Consider it like this: the Spirit within you is like an engagement ring. This solid promise expresses the existence of a union that is *real*, which God wants you to experience but has not reached complete fruition. The Spirit within you means Jesus is as close as he could possibly be—far closer than a spouse. He shares every thought and experiences every emotion. This is partly why the Spirit's intercession for us is referred to as "groanings too deep for words" (Romans 8:26). Especially as a single, it is crucial to embrace the truth of his presence with you and find ways to open yourself to this reality. During my single years, I regularly talked out loud to God when I was alone in the house or after my daughters were in bed. I needed to exercise a more demonstrative faith to help me believe. I intentionally lived as if God was real and present with me, learning to process my pain with him, not only grief but the ongoing challenges of single parenting, unsatisfied desires, and loneliness. And he was true to his word and gave me supernatural comfort and peace—*even though my circumstances didn't change.* He brought about transformation and relief by changing my heart, despite unchanging circumstances. I can testify to the truth of Psalm 28:7: "The LORD is my strength and my shield; *in him my heart trusts, and I am helped*" (emphasis added).

Despite the challenges, I want to encourage you that singleness has a place of honor in the kingdom of God. According to the Bible, you are in a position to do far more for the kingdom than those who are married. But there is something else incredibly important: your life, lived well, is a revolutionary challenge to the principalities and powers of this dark world as your obedience educates the spiritual forces of the manifold wisdom of God (see Ephesians 3:10; 6:12). Our culture is seduced by sexuality and daily sells us the lie that a life without sex is not worth living. Your commitment to live chastely as a single Christian proclaims to a watching world that there is another King, whose own willingness to embrace a different kind of life disarmed the lies of the enemy (see Colossians 2:15). You testify to the truth that sex is not necessary to have a rich, powerful life. It is an ongoing challenge to grow in learning that God's "steadfast love is better than life" (Psalm 63:3), but your life is a countercultural battle cry, not something to be pitied.

This is necessary for all Christians, but singles especially need to hold fast to the ultimate promise of a new heavens and new earth, where all tears are wiped away and every desire is fully satisfied for all eternity. For me, one amazing consequence of becoming single again was that—at least for a time—the veil between this life and the next became gloriously thin. I had a deeper sense than ever before of the brevity of this life and of the wonderful hope of the world to come. Passages like

Hebrews 11 were palpably real to me. "The world was not worthy" of those Old Testament saints who suffered through this life, believing and holding fast to the promises of God, even though they never experienced the fulfillment but only glimpsed it from afar (see Hebrews 11:38–39). And I knew this great "cloud of witnesses" (12:1) was with me, urging me, "Hang in there! Press on. It's not too much longer now and it's all worth it. He is worth it!" Like the early church, to whom the book of Hebrews was written, we need the company of the saints in order to embrace the hope before us so we do not lose heart or live for our own pleasures but for the glory of God and the good of others. This is a calling to rediscover the historic Christian faith as a life lived in self-giving hope, as foreigners and aliens in a strange land looking forward to God's promised homeland. And it demands the participation, gifts, and witness of *all* Christians.

CHAPTER 9

Sex in a Broken World

As we have seen, God's design of sex is fundamentally *good*. But the world distorts God's design, and this distortion impacts our understanding of the meaning of sexuality and how it should be expressed. This chapter focuses on the worldview behind fallen sexuality, while the next chapter will examine various sexual practices that violate God's design.

Despite the glorious truths we've considered in Genesis 1 and 2, after Adam and Eve sinned, things went downhill in every way, especially sexually. Before we are even out of Genesis, sexual practice went completely haywire. Polygamy was normalized. Visiting angels were threatened with homosexual gang rape by the men of Sodom, and Lot, Abraham's nephew, responded by offering the licentious crowd his virgin daughters (Genesis 19:1–22). Later on, Lot himself impregnates his own daughters (19:30–38). Dinah is raped, and her brothers Simeon and Levi subsequently slaughter all the males in the city (chap. 34). To top things off, the patriarch Judah is unknowingly seduced by his daughter-in-law, Tamar, who posed as a veiled prostitute because he was unwilling to fulfill his family's obligation to produce an heir (chap. 38). All this sexual craziness occurs in the first book of the Bible.

As the biblical story moves on, things did not get much better. The startling prohibitions of Leviticus 18 and 20, which forbid sex with parents, in-laws, and even grandchildren, are apparently necessary. The Bible faithfully discloses human history, exposing all its ugly warts and wrinkles. Even passages describing ardent romantic love, like Jacob's for Rachel, are sullied as Laban tricks Jacob into marrying Rachel's unloved sister, Leah, resulting in bitter rivalry and heartache (Genesis 29:1–30). The Old Testament narratives put on display the universal brokenness of humanity, slowly building to the revelation of Jesus, the light of the world, whose arrival brilliantly contrasts with the sea of humanity's darkness.

Universal Sexual Brokenness

As much as we lament our morally adrift culture, broken sexuality is not just "out there" in our decadent, post-Christian world. Homosexuality and gender confusion aren't the main problems, nor is the internet's tragic proliferation of free, hardcore porn. Neither is the church's main problem simply her silence or distorted messages. The real problem is that broken sexuality is universal, affecting every person and community on the globe.

What I mean by "broken sexuality" is that all of us have a sexuality affected by the fall. In the words of Bob Dylan, "Everything is broken."[1] Everything is tainted and out of joint. That's why Scripture says, "The whole creation has been groaning together in the pains of childbirth until now" (Romans 8:22). But things are not so broken that they do not recall their original goodness or so marred that they can't be repaired by God's grace. Though woefully fractured, humanity still bears the image of God. The fall does not mean people who do not know God can't be kind and generous. They often demonstrate tremendous acts of selflessness. Though these acts of service often generate pride in the long run. Or, because this is God's world and his governing principles still hold true, people can stumble upon the truth that joy is found by serving others instead of self. But apart from Jesus, even our "selflessness" is usually self-referential. Unless empowered by the Spirit, our actions are *never* God-referential. Paul teaches that God's wrath is coming because although humanity "knew God, they did not honor him as God or give thanks to him" but instead suppressed the truth by their unrighteousness (Romans 1:18–21). God's rightful claim is to be acknowledged as our Creator and given appropriate thanks as the One to whom we owe all things. But since the fall, humanity has chosen autonomy and rejected God.

It is important to underscore that, as a universal human condition, this brokenness impacts men *and* women. Sexual sin is a gender-neutral pathogen of the soul. Although churches increasingly acknowledge that pornography is a significant challenge to Christian men, they are still slow to see that the daughters of God also live with a broken sexuality. This can lead to even greater shame for women. One woman lamented to my colleague, "I guess I just sin more like a man." There is already so much shame surrounding sexual sin, so we need to do everything we can to invite men and women to come into the light with their struggles.

The church can't just lament a decadent culture. And we must not put our hope in trying to legislate these issues out of existence, as though politics could redeem our souls. When it comes to sexual sin, each of us has the ultimate Trojan horse beating in our chest, ready to betray us. A changed outward culture has no power to effect the deep inward transformation that is needed.

It is so important that we have a biblical understanding of humanity. Drawing out the implications of our faith for life in the twenty-first century requires being strongly rooted in the Bible's teaching so that we are able to apply its truth to the questions asked by each generation. For example, a significant argument for reconciling homosexual practice with the Christian faith is that same-sex attracted people have always felt this way. That homosexuality is *natural* for them. So Matthew Vines wrote, "Same-sex attraction is completely natural to me. It's not something I chose or something I can change."[2] The argument proceeds, if same-sex attraction is natural and not a *choice*, then it is the way God created me. Do you see the biblical hole in this logic? Although they may not say it outright, pro-gay theology is built on the inherent goodness of humanity. It asserts, "Who I am naturally is good, God-given, and should be embraced." But this is exactly the opposite of what the Bible teaches about humanity. The Bible teaches that all of us are fallen, in desperate need of redemption. Nothing short of the Son of God becoming incarnate and paying for our sin on a cursed Roman cross would suffice. The starting point of pro-gay theology is a significant departure from a Christian worldview, so it makes sense that the conclusions are inconsistent with the Bible's teaching. Just as substituting the wrong value for pi in a geometric formula would generate an incorrect answer every time.

Think about it this way—prior to coming to faith in Christ, I cheated on every woman who had the misfortune of dating me. This was *natural* to me. Wedding rings and lifelong promises went completely against the grain for me. I am not naturally monogamous. I needed a radical, supernatural intervention to become a faithful husband. (Not to mention ongoing, daily intervention by the Holy Spirit to be a loving husband and father!) A significant truth of the gospel is that humanity is irreparably broken without divine intervention. This means all of us need sexual redemption from who we are naturally. We need *new creation* in this aspect of life as much as any other. In order to understand how sexual redemption works, we need to know how sexuality is currently distorted by sin.

Sexual Scripts of the Twenty-First Century

To understand the sexual worldview of our culture, we need to acknowledge that there are certain established norms. Some Christians argue that the culture pursues sexual anarchy, but this is not strictly true. In his helpful book *Sex and the iWorld*, Dale S. Kuehne describes the three big taboos that govern secular sexual ethics in mainstream culture: first, one may not criticize or restrict another's life choices or behavior; second, one may not coerce or cause harm to another; and third, one may not engage sexually with someone without that person's consent.[3] This is important for a couple reasons: it shows that our culture does have standards. It is not a "no holds barred" sexuality, even though it is often portrayed this way by Christians. The focus on consent is important and right. But clearly this worldview places the *self* at the center—the individual is the final interpreter of ultimate truth. And truth is personal, which is why any disagreement is labeled as self-righteous and judgmental. Along with these taboos, a number of lies pervade our culture's view of sex.

The theological realities behind our image-bearing sexuality means that even under sin, sex is imbued with a certain glory. Even immorality provides the taste of transcendence. But, as with all idolatry, the gift is confused for the Giver. As a result, one of the most pervasive cultural lies is that *sex equals life*. And the flipside of this lie is that life without sex is a tragedy. Unless we engage in sexual activity, we are told we are living a pitiful existence. This is one of the key arguments in Matthew Vines's book, *God and the Gay Christian*. His starting premise is that God created him gay, and then he quickly moves to the idea that God couldn't possibly ask him to live without a romantic, sexual relationship. In a video "The Gay Debate," he describes this as a life of "forced loneliness."[4] His point is that sex and romance are so fundamental to existence and the quality of human life that no one could be reasonably expected to live without it.

It is important to note how this view undermines the significance of friendship. I have heard gay theologians boldly claim that David's lament over Jonathan demonstrates a sexual relationship: "I am distressed for you, my brother Jonathan; very pleasant have you been to me; your love to me was extraordinary, surpassing the love of women" (2 Samuel 1:26). But David was *not* saying sex with Jonathan was better than sex with women. The assertion of a sexual relationship disregards the possibility of a deep platonic friendship between men. Sadly, this exemplifies how greatly we've diminished friendship in our culture. Consider C. S. Lewis's assessment: "To the Ancients, Friendship seemed the happiest and most fully human of all loves; the crown of life and the school of virtue. The modern world, in comparison, ignores it."[5] Without having a category for deep friendship, some conclude the relationship must have been sexual, completely missing the point that David describes a friendship that transcends sex.

There is evidence for such depth of friendship even in the modern era. *All Quiet on the Western Front* tells of German soldiers in the trenches and recounts their intimacy as closer than lovers. Apparently, facing death daily and depending on your comrades for life forged a bond that felt closer than sex. But generally in our culture, same-sex friendships have diminished, especially among men. Although there has been a push in recent years to affirm the importance of friendship *within* marriage, this has contributed to the decline in emphasizing the necessity of same-sex friendships for married couples. A husband and wife should never be an island unto themselves. The burden of being "everything" to another person is more than anyone can bear.

Another big cultural lie declares *sex is just a recreational activity*. Ironically, even as many exalt sex way beyond God's design, they simultaneously weaken it by saying it's just something you do with your body with no deeper, intrinsic meaning. At best, sex is understood as a basic need, like eating and sleeping, that shouldn't carry a moral valuation. And this dovetails with autonomy, "This is *my* body—I can do with it what I please." There is no ultimate meaning to sex beyond my right to experience pleasure in the way I choose with whom I choose. This divorces procreation (and therefore the creation mandate) from sexuality. It eliminates the call to an exclusive relationship and the opportunity to be truly known by another in way that is set apart from all other relationships. It removes the focus from serving another to serving self. Reducing sex to a recreational activity trivializes the glory of knowing God's deep love for us through sexuality.

Closely related is another lie—that *sex is private*. No one has the right to say what we do in our bedrooms. In contrast, Lauren Winner writes,

> Sex is communal because it is real. Sex has conse-
> quences. Sex is dangerous and delightful and tempes-
> tuous and elemental, and it matters. What we do with
> our bodies, what we do sexually, shapes our persons.
> How we comport ourselves sexually shapes who we
> are. If we believe that sex forms us, then it goes with-
> out saying that it is public business, because how we
> build the persons we are—persons who are social and
> communal and political and economic beings—is itself
> a matter of social concern.[6]

One of the big lies with pornography is that it does not hurt anyone. But this completely ignores how the messages of pornography impact our hearts and the ways we interact with others. It is not so easy to disentangle our sexual behaviors from our thought life and personal relationships. As whole persons, behavior in one sphere of life has ripple effects to all the others. Not to mention that engagement in porn means supporting a worldwide system of injustice and oppression, not only of those directly involved in its production, but also the multitude of trafficked men and women fueled by the porn industry.

Given today's obsession with youth and beauty, the prevailing message—another lie—is that *sex appeal matters most*. It's tragic that, desperate for affirmation, young girls ask on social media, "Do you think I'm pretty or ugly?" inviting strangers to shred their sense of self.[7] The fashion industry puts beautiful people on the cover of every magazine and larger-than-life billboards. Aging celebrities defy their years with the help of injections and surgeries performed by well-paid dermatologists. All this leaves the rest of us with average looks and economic means feeling perpetually "less than." Dating apps accentuate the lie, shrinking the wondrous depth of an individual to a tiny smartphone image that invites you to "swipe right" to affirm that he or she is hot . . . or not.

Our culture prizes the exact opposite of what God values. As our Creator, he is not particularly concerned with our outward appearances. It's not as if he is delighted with how some people turned out, and then shakes his head toward others, viewing them as flawed workmanship. God's words to Samuel at the anointing of David are apt: "The LORD sees not as man sees: man looks on the outward appearance, but the LORD looks on the heart" (1 Samuel 16:7). God cares deeply about who we are on the inside, while our culture primarily appraises the outside. Speaking to wives, Peter dismisses fancy updos, lavish jewelry, and runway styles, encouraging them to "let your adorning be the hidden person of the heart with the imperishable beauty of a gentle and quiet spirit, which in God's sight is very precious" (1 Peter 3:4). This is a striking contrast to our culture, which places value on the fleeting presence of youth and beauty.

Finally, when it comes to sex, another lie is that *now matters*. People live for today, not eternity. I am not saying how we live in the present age does not matter, but the focus of the Christian life is to invest our lives in this world while looking forward to the world to come. Hebrews 11 praises the Old Testament saints for living by faith—not receiving the promises in this life but seeing them from afar and choosing to live as strangers and exiles in the present world. We are called to live today with an eye always toward *that day*.

Although there are more cultural lies surrounding sexuality, these represent some of the prevailing ideas. To sum up, the world says, "Sex is all about me!" In stark contrast to God's design, it puts the self at the center. The focus is on personal pleasure and forging one's own identity without acknowledging God and his created intent for sexuality. It misses the "profound mystery" that God longs for us to perceive through sexuality. Further, the call of Christ, to deny ourselves and take up a cross to follow him (Matthew 16:24), is completely at odds with this prevailing cultural worldview. The goal is to live for his sake and glory (see 2 Corinthians 5:14–15 and Galatians 2:20). Living sacrificially by faith means we have a hope that sustains us beyond the tangible things of this life. As we've discussed with singles and their sexuality, believing God's promises and living for the world to come sustains us through the challenge of waiting on the Lord for his blessings in the midst of disappointments. Christianity is about surrendering our supposed self-rule and submitting to Jesus as Lord.

Sex and the Allegiance of Your Heart

Because sex is ultimately about God and you, how we steward our sexuality is critical. Though physical, sex is a profoundly spiritual act that reveals the allegiance of your heart. It is ultimately a litmus test for your spirituality. Let's start by revisiting 1 Thessalonians 4:3–8:

For this is the will of God, your sanctification: that
you abstain from sexual immorality; that each one of
you know how to control his own body in holiness and
honor, not in the passion of lust like the Gentiles who
do not know God; that no one transgress and wrong
his brother in this matter, because the Lord is an
avenger in all these things, as we told you beforehand
and solemnly warned you. For God has not called us
for impurity, but in holiness. Therefore whoever disregards this, disregards not man but God, who gives his
Holy Spirit to you.

God cares about our sexuality because it is fundamentally about our relationship with him. Our sexual practice
reflects the fundamental allegiance of our hearts. This passage
articulates the simple, direct connection: God's will includes
abstaining from sexual immorality. While the Greek term
porneia stems from the root word for prostitute, it is really
an all-encompassing term used by New Testament writers to
decry any genital contact outside of God's design for marital intimacy. As mentioned previously, it refers to any type of
unchastity.

Rather than immorality, we are called to sanctification.
Sanctification is tied to the biblical term for holiness. Now,
many people conflate holiness and righteousness; believing
holiness is about morality. It is in a way, but fundamentally
holiness refers to being set apart. So when Scripture says, "God
is holy," it is referring to what theologians call the Creator-
creature distinction—the reality that God is absolutely *other*.
Similarly, we are called to sanctification and holiness as those
who are *set apart* for God. We are his people, not our own;
we've been bought with a price. Being a Christian means that
you belong to Jesus.

How you comport yourself sexually is an outward, physical manifestation of your inner spiritual reality. How we live

sexually should reflect that we're set apart, demonstrating that we belong to Jesus. Our sexuality reveals who we are in relation to our Creator. Because sexual brokenness is a universal human reality—no one *naturally* lives according to God's design—our submission to his design delineates Christians as his people. That's why Paul ends the passage with a stark warning against disregarding God.[8]

Sexual Sin Is Enslaving

Thus Paul goes on to draw a sharp distinction between Christians and Gentiles (in Greek, "the nations," meaning those outside of Christ) based on their sexual behavior. Christians, living in submission to God, "control" their bodies by the power of the Spirit. All others do what comes natural—living for their desires. If it feels good, do it! This makes sense if we are autonomous. If we do not have to answer to anyone, we might as well live however we please and enjoy the pleasure of sex with whoever is desirable to us. But this passage warns of the hook hidden in the alluring bait—when we live for our desires we become subservient to them. First Thessalonians 4:5 uses two Greek terms, *pathos* and *epithumia*, translated "passion of lust." *Pathos* refers to the passive side of vice, the suffering inherent when we are mastered by our desires. *Epithumia* is an aggressive, inordinate "ruling" desire. It enslaves. Life apart from God is shameless, wanton self-indulgence. For many people, their sexual desires become enslaving. They are completely under the control of their lusts, and their lives are built around their desperate attempt to find sexual satisfaction.

Paul's words are a fitting summary of our culture: we live "in the passion of lust like the Gentiles who do not know God." Yet rather than simply denouncing the state of culturally acceptable sexual expression, Paul's words reveal the loss that characterizes our situation. Despite the tremendous challenge of living with unsatisfied sexual desire, we're in a worse situation when we desperately attempt to satisfy them as we'll always come up empty. The hope of the gospel is that Jesus meets us in the pain of unsatisfied desires, reorienting them toward himself, because this is what all of life, including sex, is ultimately about.

Ephesians 4:19 provides a chilling insight into our enslaving desires. Describing those who do not know Christ, Paul writes, "They have become callous and have given themselves up to sensuality, greedy to practice every kind of impurity." It's like a person in cardiac arrest lying on a gurney. Sexuality becomes the defibrillator, a last desperate attempt to get life from jolts of pleasure. But the tragic irony is that the more we give ourselves over to sex, it becomes increasingly less satisfying. It becomes a case of diminishing returns. The Greek word *pleonexia*, translated "greedy," refers to utter insatiability. This insatiability leads to practicing "every kind of impurity" because the ongoing experience of dissatisfaction, despite all desperate attempts to find fulfillment, means seeking contentment in ever darker places. The tragedy of replacing God with any created thing is that the intended blessing of the gift will continually elude you. The thing you most want to embrace will keep sliding through your grasping fingers.

Sin Dehumanizes

Apart from God, we are ruled by our pleasures and driven by our instincts and desires. What does this sound like? Every other creature. As we discussed earlier, our significance as image-bearers separates us from the rest of the created order. My niece took a college course on romantic relationships. As I flipped through her textbook, I wasn't surprised to find the authors were arguing that monogamy is unnatural for humanity. Their recommendation is for couples to be honest and communicate about their open relationship, determining together the boundaries for sex with others outside of their relationship.

A friend in the Army Reserves described an occasion when his company was forced to stand at attention, overlooking a field on the parade grounds, for several long minutes. While they stood rigid, each fearful of drawing the drill sergeant's ire, two dogs wandered on to the field from opposite corners, meeting in the middle. They circled, sniffing each other, quickly mated, and continued on their way passing in opposite directions. This is how most creatures express their sexuality. But God designed us for himself with a sexuality that is distinct from the rest of the created order.

Being ruled by our natural desires is a violation of our image-bearing design. Simply put, sin makes us more *bestial*. This is why 2 Peter 2:12 describes those wantonly indulging their sinful appetites as "irrational animals, creatures of instinct" (also see Jude 10). There is a stark illustration of this in C. S. Lewis's wonderful children stories *The Chronicles of Narnia*. In his fanciful world, the Narnian animals are cognizant beings able to talk, but at the time of their creation, they were warned that if they turned away from Aslan they would lose this ability and become regular animals. This is poignantly demonstrated in the final book when Ginger the cat, a good materialist who rejects the idea of Aslan, conspires with Narnia's enemies. When confronted with the truth, he is undone and the other animals watch in horror as he loses his ability to speak, returning to a brute beast.[9] Lewis intended his readers to make the connection between the uniqueness of our humanity and our relationship to our Creator. When that is severed, our image-bearing deconstructs and we increasingly conform to the likeness of the rest of the animal kingdom.

Sexual Sin Hurts Yourself

Although there are larger societal implications for this diminishing of our humanity, the greatest cost is to the individual. This is why 1 Corinthians 6:17–18 warns, "But he who is

joined to the Lord becomes one spirit with him. Flee from
sexual immorality. Every other sin a person commits is outside the body, but the sexually immoral person sins against
his own body." Paul is not saying that sexual immorality is
somehow worse than other sins. The list of seven abominable
things that God really hates in Proverbs 6:16–19 have nothing to do with sex. Sexual immorality is not a worse sin,
but it is more personally destructive. Sexual sin damages the
self in a way that is unique, unlike any other sin. Why? Paul
points to the profound mystery, reminding that sexuality is a
reflection of the ultimate union with Jesus. Sexual sin dilutes
the greatest wonder in the universe. The glorious hope of the
world to come is living in a face-to-face relationship with
Jesus—of which marriage and sexuality is the closest terres-
trial analogy.

Sexual sin is against ourselves because God entrusts us
with a precious gift as sexual beings. As discussed in the last
chapter, even unsatisfied desires can lead to deeper intimacy
with him when we understand that our longings reflect his
heart for us. For married people, the invitation to relational
oneness and deeper *knowing* is woefully diminished when
this gift is dragged through the town square. And the gift is
intended to lead to deeper awe as the years together lengthen.
There are whispers of the divine in the heady rush of love's
first bloom, but the full-throated angelic chorus grows over
the decades of experience, shared loves, and heartaches. This
increasing knowledge is designed to produce a growing tenderness and softness that enhances sexual intimacy. The point
isn't the pleasure but the person and the way this earthly relationship mirrors the consummation of the great marriage yet
to be. Although sexual sin has power to enslave, often with
painful consequences, it is the loss of the *blessing* of godly
sexuality that makes this sin profoundly against self.

Sexual Sin Hurts Others

Because sexuality is a signpost to God's exclusive love for us, he takes it seriously. That's why he uses stern warnings for those who engage others in sexual immorality. First Thessalonians 4:6 exhorts "that no one transgress and wrong his brother in this matter, because the Lord is an avenger in all these things, as we told you beforehand and solemnly warned you." Paul makes clear that immorality is not a victimless sin, even when both are consenting adults. Because sexuality points to our ultimate union, it wields devastating power when we sin against another. The intended glory of sexuality is reflected even in the broken shards of its wreckage. The term *transgressing* has in view trampling down an established safeguard or boundary. Further, *wronging another* is commerce language, expressing that immorality *defrauds* others. In sexual sin, we are ripping someone off, trespassing on another's soul. When we sin sexually against another—and I particularly have sexual abuse in mind, though the passage is not that specific—it is trespassing on another's personhood and robbing them of gifts given by God himself. This is a serious and terrible transgression—against those made and loved by God. The warning is severe because God wants to woo *his beloved* through this good gift. He wants to offer himself, but when we live as Gentiles, we are drawing one another away from life with Christ.

So, Paul makes a dire pronouncement—Jesus will be an avenger. In the Bible, an avenger is one who brings justice and freedom for the oppressed, one who redeems and restores when life has been taken away. If you have been sinned against sexually, hear these words! Jesus takes seriously the abuse you have suffered and promises to avenge. Sexual abuse is perhaps the most horrific trauma anyone can endure and this passage makes clear that Jesus cares about what happened to you and he will make it right.

The most glorious depiction of Jesus as an avenger is in Revelation 19:11–21. He is pictured as the ultimate archetype of the hero on a white horse! And his name is "Faithful and True" (v. 11). This passage foretells the last day when Jesus storms out of heaven on a warhorse, followed closely by the armies of heaven. The beast and false prophet gather with the kings of this world to make their feeble stand. Do you know what happens? Jesus kills everyone! The hosts of heaven only come to watch and cheer. The One who is our ultimate Bridegroom is also the champion who fights on our behalf, bringing justice and vengeance on our enemies. "The rest were slain by the sword that came from the mouth of him who was sitting on the horse, and all the birds were gorged with their flesh" (v. 21). The abuse you suffered has robbed you of life and God's promise is that he will settle the score with your abuser and restore life to you. Please trust him to do this! Please know he understands your pain—he is the God who suffered!—and promises that he will set all things right.

If you are a survivor of sexual abuse, I understand that it is painful to be told that sex is a good gift. This has not been your experience. Often with abuse, it was someone's very first sexual experience that was so profoundly broken. I pray that you will know that God cares about what happened to you and promises to make things right. He deeply cares about the pain you have suffered. He weeps with you and promises vengeance and complete restoration. If you are looking for resources, one of the most helpful and accessible is *On the Threshold of Hope* by Diane Langberg.[10] But as Diane recommends, examining these things is a journey best embarked upon with a wise, experienced counselor.

Further, 1 Corinthians 6:15 warns, "Do you not know that your bodies are members of Christ? Shall I then take the members of Christ and make them members of a prostitute? Never!" This passage indicates that there are communal, spiritual implications to seemingly private sexual sin. As we are called to be one body, inextricably linked together, our maturity is dependent on one another, and our sexuality impacts the health and growth of others (see Ephesians 4:15–16).

Sex and the New Creation

Part of the reason why there's so much confusion about sexuality in the church is because we have lost focus on the big picture of God's story. God had a plan for his world at the time of creation. He made all things and declared his handiwork "very good" (Genesis 1:31). Humanity was created in God's image, to serve as his stewards—wise rulers over the rest of the created order. But humanity's rebellion resulted in the curse of sin, so everything is now tainted and subject to death, bondage, and corruption. Jesus entered into this mess, declaring the arrival of the kingdom of God and reversing the curse through miraculous healings, ruling over the forces of nature, and even raising the dead. Through Jesus's death, the record of debt against us because of our sin was nailed to the cross so that we could be reconciled to God (see Colossians 2:13–15; 2 Corinthians 5:17–19). The New Testament designates Jesus as the "new Adam," and the description of his exaltation and rule over creation places him in the role intended for humanity (Romans 5:12–21). As such, Jesus's followers are now the true humanity "in Christ." The goal of his followers is to work toward God's intentions for his creation, even though our work will always be partial prior to Jesus's return and the creation of the new heavens and new earth. This is why his followers are called to deny themselves and take up their cross, giving away their wealth and pouring out their lives for his kingdom.

When we lose focus on God's bigger cosmic purposes in redemption, we tend toward a very individualistic outlook. As Christians, we need to have a bigger perspective on the kingdom of God. God's good creation had a vision that was headed somewhere, namely God's image-bearers extending his gracious rule to all creation until the knowledge of the glory of God covers the earth as the waters cover the sea (Habakkuk 2:14). The fall derailed everything, leading to a fundamental disordering of the world and our desires.[11] But Jesus's establishment of the kingdom of God reasserts the Father's righteous rule over the wayward world of darkness. This is why gender is central to God's design for sexuality. When God created the world, he established intentional order to it. We need to fight against the "expressive individualism" of our current culture that rejects the good order of God's creation and his loving rule overall.

Despite the current brokenness, Scripture anticipates the overturning of the curse and the renewal of creation. Consider the picture given in Ezekiel 47. In an amazing vision of the coming kingdom, the prophet sees a trickle of water flowing from the temple. He follows it fifteen thousand feet, and sees it has grown to a torrent, ankle-deep. Successively measuring the same length, it is then up to his knees, then his waist, and finally a roaring river no one can pass through. The river grows, rushing in its course, and eventually plunges into the Dead Sea which suddenly swarms with all kinds of fish. One of the most desolate places on earth explodes with life. Fisherman line the beach that once was only a salt wasteland. The prophet concludes, "On the banks, on both sides of the river, there will grow all kinds of trees for food. Their leaves will not wither, nor their fruit fail, but they will bear fresh fruit every month, because the water for them flows from the sanctuary. Their fruit will be for food, and their leaves for healing" (v. 12). Do not be disheartened, the kingdom is coming with a fullness we can't begin to imagine. And just as the Dead Sea teems with life, so your sexuality will be gloriously transformed and fully redeemed!

CHAPTER 10

Sex Against God's Design

In a fallen world where all of humanity is dealing with a broken sexuality, there are all kinds of sexual expressions that do not fit the pattern of God's creation. The cultural cacophony combined with the church's silence means there is significant confusion in the body of Christ. The goal of this chapter is not to discuss every possible sexual expression but to examine a sampling of the most prominent behaviors that do not fit God's design. Although Scripture does not exhaustively address every possible ethical conundrum, its principles provide a framework to address every issue confronting the human condition.

Masturbation

In 1992, I was a college student when the TV series *Seinfeld* aired the infamous masturbation episode. I remember watching it with about a dozen friends, all of us crammed in front of an old tube TV, staring at the small screen. This private, embarrassing activity was on prime-time television, with even a female character acknowledging her participation. It was hilarious and liberating. Afterwards, we dispersed amid exuberant chatter. A lot has changed since 1992, and now this behavior is incredibly normalized and mainstream. Once a source of personal shame, masturbation is now embraced as a healthy sexual outlet, especially for singles. This idea has even infiltrated the church. Although there is much to commend in Allender and Longman's *God Loves Sex*, I was disheartened by their embrace of masturbation as a commendable behavior. They asked, "What is the difference between masturbation that is full of lust and self-pleasuring that is full of goodness?"[1] Although they quickly identify the sinfulness of lust and pornography, they fail to make a clear case for the goodness of masturbation.

Evangelicals have wrestled for years over whether masturbation is a sin, with prominent voices on both sides. The debate exists largely because it is an activity that is not condemned by a clear biblical proof text.[2] Although I can't point you to a specific chapter and verse forbidding this behavior, a robust understanding of God's design for sexuality, coupled with the awareness of what it means to be a disciple of Jesus, makes clear there is no room for masturbation in the life of a Christian. Most Christian leaders who affirm the practice point to the absence of a biblical prohibition and acknowledge their reticence to call people to the pain of living with unsatisfied sexual desires. Allender and Longman said, "To tell singles not to desire sex or to forbid the poetic anticipation of it before marriage is to ask them to betray the way God made them. In other words, it is asking the impossible and the undesirable."[3] While the call to refrain from masturbation can be a hard teaching and no tenderhearted pastor wants to call his people to unnecessary suffering, refusing to label solo sex as sin invites singles into behavior that misses the mark for God's design for sexuality.

We've explored that human sexuality is about deeper truths, not simply permissible and out-of-bounds behaviors. There are two main principles that clearly exclude masturbation: first, because of our image-bearing, sexual activity is always reserved for marriage because it is inherently relational, designed to cultivate deep intimacy with another. Second, as we saw from 1 Corinthians 7:1–5, the goal of sex in marriage is selfless service—the pleasuring of another. Obviously, masturbation fails on both counts. As a solitary activity, it is not rooted in relationship. There is no opportunity for deepening intimacy and knowing another. Further, far from selfless service, it is a picture of living for self. Masturbation asks, "Why should I have to wait if I can have this pleasure now?" This attitude is counter to Jesus's call of discipleship where self-denial is central. Allender and Longman are clear that lust is sinful, but their idea of singles having a sanctified imagination about a future spouse is an unrealistic and idealized concept that's disconnected from the actual practice of masturbation. Further, their argument is built on the prolonged singleness of typical Americans, rather than a careful application of Scripture.

God designed sexuality to be like every other aspect of the Christian life—turning away from selfish desires in order to honor God with our bodies and use them to serve one another. We explored the importance of this in the expression of marital sexuality, but this principle extends to all of the Christian life. Multiple passages proclaim that Christianity frees us from living for ourselves. We live for Christ first, and to love and bless others second (see 2 Corinthians 5:14–15; Galatians 2:20; Philippians 2:3–4; 1 Peter 4:1–5). Jesus promises that when we live according to this pattern we truly find *life*. (All four Gospels include this central teaching: Matthew 10:39; Mark 8:35; Luke 9:24; and John 12:25.) Living for ourselves guarantees that true life and peace will forever slip through our fingers. As we saw in the last chapter, this is particularly true of our sexuality.

There are practical considerations here as well. Even apart from the clear evils of porn or sexual fantasy, masturbation will likely reinforce our natural, self-focused bent. If the Lord provides a spouse, a history of solo sex may make it difficult to approach the marriage bed looking to selflessly serve another

because masturbation is focused exclusively on personal gratification. Admittedly, all couples need to grow in practicing
God-honoring, selfless sex, but since masturbation is by definition practiced by yourself and for yourself, it's setting a pattern of sexual gratification that is self-focused—which is not
God's design for expressing our sexuality.

Similarly, a married person is defrauding his or her spouse
through masturbation. A healthy sex life takes work, requiring
selfless emotional and spiritual investment, as well as learning to physically serve someone built very differently than
yourself. Learning to give pleasure to each other in physical
intimacy is an outward manifestation of how a couple is to
grow in their knowing of each other emotionally and spiritually. Their sexual differences are part of the joy and wonder
that point to the greater reality of union with Christ, who is
radically other. Masturbation selfishly takes the easy road of
personal gratification at the cost of deepening oneness and
intimacy in marriage.

This raises an additional issue. Is it okay for couples to uti-
lize technology to have virtual sex with each other? Although
some Christians have supported the activity, this again distorts the design to selflessly serve one another. The goal is to be
together, united physically, as well as emotionally and spiritually. Practically, God created sexual satisfaction to be a kind
of relational glue in marriage. Only my spouse can provide
this amazing pleasure. It is a unique gift that binds us together
because each is dependent on the other for its provision. It
requires a spouse to generously give of himself or herself. Even
if your spouse is eager for you to experience pleasure remotely,
you can't escape the reality that you are alone in the room,
ultimately pleasuring yourself. Self-stimulation by definition is
focused on me, even if your spouse is on the other end of the
phone or FaceTime.

And that highlights another problem. Many Christians
justify masturbation because our culture elevates sexual desire

to a physical need. But the hard truth is that no one has ever died because they didn't have sex (unlike oxygen, water, food, shelter). This is *not* to say that living with unsatisfied sexual desires is easy! We should have great compassion for singles living in celibate faithfulness to Christ and couples languishing in sexless marriages. But the reality is that sex is a wonderful blessing—a good gift from God—but it is not a source of life in and of itself.

Most secular therapists agree that masturbation is a means of self-soothing and finding comfort. This is actually one of the key problems. As a teen in a substance-abuse-recovery facility, I was encouraged by my therapist to masturbate for stress relief. Although this may be the lesser of two evils for a teen with addictions, it is not the most helpful solution. And while masturbation and pornography do not always go together, they frequently *are* associated, and both are addictive and destructive to relationships.

Here's the crux of the issue: God declares himself to be the "God of all comfort" (2 Corinthians 1:3–4). He wants to meet us in our sadness, loneliness, and frustration. He promises to satisfy "you with good so that your youth is renewed like the eagle's" (Psalm 103:5). Jesus promised the Holy Spirit would be our Comforter (John 15:26, KJV). There is a danger when we turn elsewhere to soothe the ache in our soul. Jonah 2:8 warns, "Those who cling to worthless idols turn away from God's love for them" (NIV). When we embrace false and fleeting comforts to satisfy our deep, spiritual longings, we will not find lasting contentment or a balm for our yearnings.

We should seek comfort in ways that can facilitate deepening fellowship with God (such as a walk in the woods, enjoying nutritious food, warm conversation with friends). A helpful gauge of whether your pursuit of comfort is drawing you closer to the Giver or not is the lens of Colossians 3:17, "And whatever you do, whether in word or deed, do everything in the name of the Lord Jesus, giving thanks to God the

Father through him." Does masturbation invite you to engage God and give thanks to him?

Wise Christians will tread this road carefully—as has been done historically, we don't want to heap shame on those struggling with masturbation. If we are honest, the issue is virtually universal for all of us at some point in our lives. This should mean we show compassion as those who can empathize. But we never want to shrink back from calling out sin for what it is and inviting people to return to their first love—the One who promises pleasure forevermore at his right hand (Psalm 16:11).

Pornography

Pornography has been around a long time. In college I had the amazing opportunity of spending a semester studying in Rome. One weekend I took a day trip down to the ruins of Pompeii. I was astounded and delighted (pagan that I was) to find pornographic frescoes that survived Vesuvius. I don't know if they're the oldest porn in existence, but at nearly two thousand years old, it has got to be close. In the modern world, changes in imaging technology, especially in the last century, were fueled by the porn industry. What has emerged in the digital age of high-speed internet is a rampaging monster. It's also a tsunami of spiritual destruction among men and women in the church. One pastor shared that the elders in his church used to complain that he talked too much about porn in his sermons. But when they started assisting him with counseling crisis marriages, they realized how pervasive the problem is. Again, this is a gender-neutral problem. One woman frantically pulled me aside as I was leaving a speaking event at a church to discuss with me her twelve-year-old daughter's struggle with internet porn. The mother had just discovered that it'd been going on for months.

Pornography violates God's design in all kinds of ways. First, it teaches that sex and personal pleasure are the most important experiences of life and that this pleasure is a fundamental right and should be obtained at any cost. Therefore, it is a poignant picture of exploitation. Its very essence is to make others subservient to *your* pleasure. Image-bearers are turned into commodities and profoundly diminished as individuals. Porn literally reduces people to larger-than-life body parts that exist for personal pleasure.

While porn disconnects the act of sex from a relationship of love and respect, it also encourages aggression and abuse. There is a reason why consent has become such a big issue in our time. Some have described a "rape culture" on college campuses because young men, raised on porn since elementary school, have lost any sense of appropriate boundaries. I have even read articles encouraging young men to talk to their consenting partners before choking them during intercourse. It is hard to imagine that such distorted, horrific behaviors surrounding sex would need to be addressed, but the proliferation of free, hard-core porn has normalized criminal behaviors, such as assault, during sex. In addition to this terrible reality, many women who have entered the porn industry came from broken family situations or are survivors of childhood sexual abuse. We are also learning that some women involved with porn have been trafficked. Far from a victimless crime, users of pornography take part in a profound institutional evil that God hates, and Jesus promises to be an avenger of the oppressed.

As described in the last chapter discussing Ephesians 4:19, porn tends to spiral downward with increasing depravity. What used to satisfy eventually satiates no longer. Like all addictions, when we give ourselves over to sensuality it means we will be confronted with diminishing returns. Many people have experienced this as pornographic images that once excited become bland. The search begins for more stimulating fodder. What began with swimsuit and underwear ads turns to full nudity, then increasingly graphic depictions of sexual

activity, swerving toward greater perversity. The universal cultural slide toward darker sexuality was profoundly illustrated
in the wide embrace of *Fifty Shades of Grey* as BDSM went
mainstream. The darkest diabolical forces are at work in the
enslaving power of porn's increasing depravity.

Of course, masturbation is typically the end goal of pornography use. It is critical to realize that internet porn is a
whole new beast that even secular researchers are beginning
to acknowledge as deeply problematic. One troubling outcome
is that men in their twenties and thirties are the largest growing demographic of men struggling with erectile dysfunction.[4]
Young men are so programmed by the constant novelty and
millions of partners available online that a real woman is not
as exciting. One young man, struggling sexually in his new
marriage, described his use of internet porn as an à la carte
menu—"Tonight I'll have some of this and this and a little of
that . . ." No single individual can compete with the composite
of hundreds of others. For many, internet porn becomes an
enslaving addiction coupled with the false comfort of solo sex.
The challenge of negotiating real life with an actual person
can make porn an ever more attractive alternative for sexual
release. And the technicolor intoxication of that false reality
as a coping mechanism for the challenges of life in a fallen
world can lead to a destructive, addictive cycle with orgasm's
chemical pleasure driving the train.

God intends sex to happen in the context of selflessness,
mutual love, and affirmation expressed within the deep safety
of a committed, lifelong relationship. Pornography shatters
every aspect of what God intends. And the accompanying lifestyle of lies and deceit completely erodes the foundation for
marital trust.

Before my first sexual experience as a teen, I had been
exposed to a lot of pornography. The hard-core videos I
watched at friends' houses on VHS tapes were the most destructive. Even though TVs in the eighties weren't the wide-screen

behemoths of today, watching porn still made sexual body parts literally larger than life. I was so impacted by these things that my first girlfriend commented on my attention to her body parts instead of *her*.

Sex Outside Marriage

Sex outside the marriage covenant, either as fornication, if single, or adultery, if married, violates God's design in significant ways. First John 5:2 teaches "By this we know that we love the children of God, when we love God and obey his commandments." Inasmuch as God's will for sexuality is clearly presented in Scripture, when we engage in sexual sin with another person it is a profoundly unloving act. It causes a breach in the most important relationship that exists. True love looks like doing everything we can to facilitate for one another a deepening of that ultimate relationship with God, rather than hindering it. Sexual sin with another steers that person away from the only true source of life and down a dark path that leads to destruction. When unmarried couples argue for the acceptance of their sexual behavior because they deeply love each other but marriage is not currently expedient, they are using a definition of love that is completely foreign to the Bible.

We've already discussed at length that the Bible is extremely positive about the place of romance and erotic passion, but when it talks about *love* there is much more in view than fervent emotion. In addition to stressing that love for another person flows from our love for God, the Bible describes love in terms of action. Consider 1 Corinthians 13:4–6, "Love is patient and kind; love does not envy or boast; it is not arrogant or rude. It does not insist on its own way; it is not irritable or resentful; it does not rejoice at wrongdoing, but rejoices with the truth." Biblical love has nothing to do with the way a person makes you feel, and everything to do with how you treat that person.

This means you shouldn't call another to be naked and vulnerable with you physically—the most poignant picture of giving possible with your body—until you have committed yourself wholly to that individual. So, the biggest violation is attempting to experience all the blessings of a sexual union without the commitment. And this is true even if both partners are mutually *ambivalent* about that commitment. Because God designed us as fully integrated physical and spiritual beings, the physiology of sex (particularly oxytocin as discussed earlier) can result in a sense of bonding even though true commitment is absent. This accentuates the pain when relationships fall apart. Although there is no guarantee that even committed marriages will not end in failure, unmarried romantic relationships are far less secure. For those who live outside of a marriage promise, it is brutal to experience one of the deepest expressions of *knowing*, only to be ultimately rejected.

This heartbreaking experience makes a mockery of the deep love God wants you to experience through your sexuality. He wants the sweet affirmation of marital intimacy to be a window into his heart for you. But when sex is expressed wrongly, that picture can be swallowed by shame. Sex with someone outside a marital covenant takes a precious gift that's imbued with spiritual power and damages it. Only sex practiced in an exclusive relationship built on the foundation of promises genuinely points to the profound mystery of Christ and his church.

The most horrific breakdown of God's design is adultery There is a reason why this is the behavior God uses to agonizingly illustrate his personal pain in idolatry. One of the hardest aspects of ministry for me is working with spouses who have suffered infidelity, which obliterates the safety and security of their marriage. It is a pain I can't begin to imagine. I am honored to walk with men and women who have suffered this profound injustice and who continue to cling to the one who is called "Faithful and True" (Revelation 19:11).

Gay Marriage

The pro-gay theology movement put out a pamphlet many years ago. The cover read, "Everything Jesus ever said about homosexuality." When you opened it, the inside was blank, sending a clear message that Jesus said nothing about homosexuality, so it's a nonissue. There are at least two problems here. First, arguments from silence are often erroneous. It is true that we have no teachings of Jesus that deal specifically with homosexuality. But the same goes for incest, bestiality, rape, spousal abuse, and more. His silence on a specific topic does not logically imply that it is inconsequential to him or that he disagrees with a clear teaching from the Old Testament (in the case of homosexual behavior, see Leviticus 18:22 and 20:13). Silence does not equal tacit approval. To the contrary, Jesus's teaching affirms the Law:

> "Do not think that I have come to abolish the Law or the Prophets; I have not come to abolish them but to fulfill them. For truly, I say to you, until heaven and earth pass away, not an iota, not a dot, will pass from the Law until all is accomplished. Therefore whoever relaxes one of the least of these commandments and teaches others to do the same will be called least in the kingdom of heaven, but whoever does them and teaches them will be called great in the kingdom of heaven." (Matthew 5:17–19)

Second, as we have seen, Jesus affirmed God's creational design in his discussion of divorce in Matthew 19:3–12. His point is that heterosexual, lifelong monogamy rooted in covenantal promises is God's sexual template for partnered human beings.

In the last chapter, I briefly addressed some of the problems with pro-gay theology. In addition to the exegetical gymnastics required to work around the biblical prohibitions,[5] the very starting point is flawed, for it asserts the inherent goodness of "natural" desire. The importance of understanding the gospel as the message of God's coming cosmic renewal helps to orient us to appropriate kingdom principles. As mentioned above, promises and lifelong fidelity are incredibly important boundaries for a sexual relationship. But they are not the only conditions. Advocates for gay marriage argue that gender does not really matter. But the two big picture theological truths—that gender is a window into differentiation within the Godhead and that marriage is about Christ and the church—demand a heterosexual union. When the union is homosexual, there is no profound mystery. There is no sense of wonder at being united with someone fundamentally other as there is with a husband and wife. A same-sex couple cannot mirror the profound mystery of Christ and his church.

Most Christians who have been persuaded away from the church's historic understanding of this issue have not come to their conclusion on primarily theological or biblical grounds. Rather, personal stories of same-sex attraction have shaped their perspective on the issue. It is important to acknowledge same-sex attracted people haven't willfully chosen a "lifestyle." Their desires emerged unbidden, usually with profound fear and shame. Many have always felt this way, often suffering in silence. And many who were raised in the church have felt condemned for years. Not to mention the tragic tales of bullying and abuse. In the face of such crushing psychological and spiritual trauma, it is no wonder that many have embraced a theology that seems to grant relief.

Such experiences call for deep compassion. We should be committed to justice and to teaching our children to defend the weak and ridiculed, even at personal cost. We need to make sure the gospel of grace is proclaimed every week in our churches and that Jesus is exalted as the glorious Savior whose sacrifice covers all sin, so no one walks away feeling condemned. And we need to talk more about the reality of same-sex attraction within Christian experience so that our many sisters and brothers wrestling with this issue do not feel so alone. But we can't alter the clear teaching of Scripture. As hard as it may be, we need to stand by what the Bible says about our sexuality. Anything less is a rejection of God's truth and profoundly unloving, since it directs people to find solace for their troubles somewhere other than Jesus.

When I first showed up as an intern at Harvest USA nearly twenty years ago, it was because I had a heart for the gay community. Unlike most Christians of my generation, homosexuality was not a nameless, faceless evil perpetuated by caricatures from gay pride parades. As a waiter in downtown Philadelphia in the early nineties, I developed friendships with a number of gay men. This was prior to coming to faith in Jesus, so, as a college student who drank too much, I welcomed the opportunity to go out after work with a few coworkers to a local gay bar—proud to be such a progressive, straight male. But as I developed friendships with these men, I heard their stories. Many said, "I always wanted a family. I love kids. I never asked for this. If you could put a pill on this bar that would make me straight, I'd take it!" But they lamented further that they'd tried everything—therapy, "religion," straight porn. Nothing had taken away their desires. Although embracing the gay life was not their first or best choice, it seemed their only option. These conversations, even as a sodden unbeliever, stuck with me and eventually led me to the doors of Harvest USA. This was not how these men *wanted* to live. They longed for a different life, but it seemed unattainable. I do not believe God promises to take away our temptations, but I know he offers us grace to live differently.[6]

I realize that same-sex attraction may be an issue for many readers. So I want to make it clear that all sexuality is broken and disjointed. Heterosexuality is not pure just because it boasts the right configuration of body parts. Remember, sexual brokenness is universal for humanity. All forms of sexuality outside God's design need redemption in Christ. And he is faithful. He will keep his promise to bring us safely through this life and into his coming kingdom with great joy. There is a day coming when all our disordered desires—no matter which direction they're bent—will be forever set right.

The Issue of Transgender

The relativizing of gender has become even more pronounced with the surging transgender phenomenon of recent years. Although this has been an issue for people for a very long time, the increase in cultural acceptance has led to an explosion of gender confusion. It's important to note that many gender-dysphoric people have suffered with profound distress for a long time. The last thing I want to do is dismiss the reality of their pain. It is real and requires care and intervention. But I want to consider how this issue further erodes God's design and is in fact a disastrous instance of the growing expressive individualism in our culture.

The massive confusion in our culture about sex and gender is increased by the airtime this issue receives in the media. When I met her, my wife was a middle school English teacher. The last year she taught, the newly minted Gay-Straight Alliance Club put posters all around the school. The top said, *Don't think like this:* and showed the traditional male and female bathroom stick figures, blue and pink respectively. The bottom said, *Think like this:* and depicted half a dozen permutations of gender pairings and colorings. I understand the need to rebuff caricatures of male and female stereotypes. Christians must remember that God delights in diversity and created the billions of utterly unique individuals currently inhabiting the planet, many of whom will not fall into the gender stereotypes of their specific cultures. But the middle school poster was a stark depiction of confusion that dismissed the right ordering of the cosmos in favor of chaos.

This confusion about sex and gender is making major inroads into the church. In the wake of the church's silence over sexuality and the growing biblical ignorance among American Christians, I understand how some are confused over the issue of gay marriage. The stories we hear from loved ones are compelling. We want them to be happy and to find romantic love. Though a lie, it can seem plausible that all God really cares about is love and monogamy and that we do not need to get hung up about gender. But it is astounding that many Christians embrace the entire LGBTQ+ acronym. Transgender is not just about sexual ethics. It calls into question the very character of God as a wise, loving, good Creator who knows what he is doing when he particularly knits together each individual in his or her mother's womb (see Psalm 139:13–16). Accepting the transgender argument is to flatly say God, who is all-knowing, made a mammoth mistake when he made some people. It is a "no confidence" vote in his goodness and wisdom. I understand that people without faith would make that argument. But it makes absolutely no sense coming from those who claim to follow the true King. Christians affirming transgender is a new depth of embracing expressive individualism.

People in and outside the church are undermining created gender distinctions with an appeal to science. Beyond the anecdotal evidence of transgender stories, the "scientific" argument is based on the intersex condition, which is usually caused by chromosomal disorders resulting in ambiguous genitalia. It is not immediately clear whether the individual is male or female. This occurs in less than one of twenty thousand births. Now, the fact that this happens to anyone is tragic and should elicit tender compassion. Jesus seems to have addressed this reality when he taught "there are eunuchs who have been so from birth" (Matthew 19:12). But it's critically important to remember that we do not determine what is normative based on circumstances clearly classified as disorders. It is illogical to disregard the male/female gender binary because 0.005 percent of the population is nonconforming due to a chromosomal disorder. We should be heartbroken that the fall is so devastating that it extends all the way down to our genetic data, but we shouldn't be evaluating what is right, healthy, and good based on the existence of brokenness in a fallen world.

I fear the coming consequences resulting from the push for wholesale acceptance of the transgender narrative, including children at younger and younger ages. There is incredible backlash from LGBTQ+ rights groups when the media dares to publish an article suggesting some teens may latch onto transgender as the answer to the universal experience of tween-identity angst only to grow out of that phase.[7] Parents, overzealous to appear affirming and loving, allow preschool children to make decisions that will ripple through the rest of their lives.

The transgender narrative leads to a breakdown of God's design for sexuality. It is a rejection of God's creation of the individual and the declaration of his handiwork as very good. Part of our gospel hope is that we are adopted into God's family (see John 1:12–13). He becomes our Father and gives us his name. To be transgender, on the other hand, is a picture of an orphan, desperate for identity and forced to find a name for self, because he or she cannot rest in the goodness of the Creator. Individuals who reject their natural gender essentially oppose God's creative choice, turning away from God's wisdom to assert their own.

In our culture, it is possible to be biologically male yet claim a female gender and desire a "heterosexual" relationship with a man—a relationship presumably including sexual activity that's labeled heterosexual, though there are no female body parts. Or the same individual could desire a lesbian relationship, in which case they'd be engaged in gay sex with heterosexual body parts. I'm highlighting this only to demonstrate that there is massive confusion. Some schools and businesses start every meeting by going around the table so each individual can establish his or her preferred pronouns so that everyone is on the same page. I realize for some, gender dysphoria has been a source of deep pain for decades, but others are now questioning their gender who previously might have never thought to do so. These are confusing, troubling times in which our image-bearing sexuality is radically undermined.

Universal Sexual Brokenness

While many Christians are understandably alarmed by the sweeping cultural changes of the last decade or so—and while I myself have been detailing these problems as *cultural* problems—we need to focus on the redemption of our *own* sexualities! Although Christians should seek to offer a public witness to Christ, we should never put our hope in legislating change. The Bible teaches that we do not wage war as the world does, but our weapons are *spiritual* with power to *demolish strongholds* (see 2 Corinthians 10:3–6). How does the kingdom go forward? It goes forward individually as people come to faith and receive the transforming power of the Spirit's indwelling. As individuals focus on personal holiness, together in the community of the local church, the result is a growing corporate witness that can be culturally transformative.

If you are overwhelmed by our culture's decadence, I have two encouragements for you. First, and most importantly, Jesus promised to build his church and that the gates of hell would not prevail against it (Matthew 16:18). You can stake everything on that! Despite the immorality of our culture, it still looks pretty tame compared to the first-century Greco-Roman world in which the kingdom went forward with power. And that brings us to the second point. Only revival will turn the tide in our culture. And revival always begins with the church of Jesus Christ coming to deeper repentance and returning to him as our first love. My hope in writing this book is that through your sexuality you will have a grander view of his heart for you. That you will be amazed afresh by the wonder of his love and see him not simply as the Savior who loves sinners, but as a lover who's enthralled with his beloved and looking forward with great delight to the coming wedding day.

In the meantime, focus on your own sexual redemption. Like me, that will keep you plenty busy. And if you have already made great strides there, ask God what new ethical issues he'd like to tackle in your life. Although God's answer to our prayers is often "wait," here is one prayer he answers right away, "Search me, O God, and know my heart! Try me and know my thoughts! And see if there be any grievous way in me, and lead me in the way everlasting!" (Psalm 139:23–24). May we heed the following words in expectation of God's transformative work in our hearts and in our culture, "Beloved, I urge you as sojourners and exiles to abstain from the passions of the flesh, which wage war against your soul. Keep your conduct among the Gentiles honorable, so that when they speak against you as evildoers, they may see your good deeds and glorify God on the day of visitation" (1 Peter 2:11–12).

CHAPTER 11

Parenting Challenges
and Opportunities

Parents in the twenty-first century are facing significant challenges that were previously unknown. Everything from the explosion of technology, which makes hard-core pornography readily available, to the inroads of the LGBTQ+ movement in media, entertainment, and schools. Parenting these days is not for the faint of heart! But it is absolutely critical to enter in to conversations with your kids, no matter how uncomfortable. When I speak in churches, I regularly ask how many people in attendance were raised in a Christian home where sexuality was discussed. Typically, less than 10 percent had Christian parents who explained sexuality. And most of the 10 percent had a book given to them without further engagement.

Christian parents can no longer afford to be passive on sexuality. You must see this—if you are silent, the culture is eager to swoop in and disciple your child sexually! If you do not proactively engage your kids on issues of sexuality, you are abdicating a crucial aspect of parenting. Kids desperately need to be shepherded in this important area of life.

For many parents, this is extremely difficult. It is hard for a whole host of reasons, but loving your kids means getting outside your comfort zone. Either you face the awkward conversations, or you leave your kids to sort out the lies of the world on their own. Trust me, if you are silent with your kids on this issue, the painful fallout in their lives will far outweigh the embarrassment and discomfort you will experience in helping them think through their sexuality in a godly way.

It is also important to realize this issue is too big for individual families to combat on their own. Christian parents need the support of the entire body of Christ. Churches must begin addressing these challenges and providing support to parents. Trying to fight single-handedly against the sexual onslaught of our culture is too much for any family. This is true for all of us, but it is incredibly important for single parents. The sexual "principalities and powers" of this current evil age are a force that only the united church can withstand. But however daunting the challenge may be, remember Jesus's encouragement: "I have said these things to you, that in me you may have peace. In the world you will have tribulation. But take heart; I have overcome the world" (John 16:33).

How Are *You* Doing?

We have covered that sexual brokenness is universal. This really matters for you as a parent. Your own growth in sexual redemption will affect how you address sexuality with your kids. Are there skeletons from your sexual past that you are hiding from your spouse or Christian friends? What about current struggles with lust or porn? Any time there is unconfessed sin—past or present—we live under guilt and shame. And guilt and shame always impact current relationships. Your own unresolved struggles in these areas will either keep you silent or cause you to present a distorted message about sexuality to your kids. I would urge you to address whatever areas of your past or present still require sexual redemption.

If you have been sinned against sexually, it is critical to seek a wise and *experienced* therapist to help you process this trauma. Sexual abuse is one of the most painful human experiences, and we need others to help us work through it. It is true that there will always be scars, but deep healing for your soul is possible, and it is so important to make sure distorted views of sex coming out of your experience are not passed on to your children.

Where are you in the fight against the world's lies? Are you wrestling with whether homosexuality is a sin? How has Hollywood impacted your view of romance and sexuality? Or "Christian romance" novels? When you are in a hard place in your marriage, the sickly, sweet completely unrealistic messages of romantic comedies can be really unhelpful. There are voices shaping our expectations of romance and sexuality that too often go unchecked.

Of course, coming from another angle, our culture communicates that marriage kills good sex. It turns sex into an idol, stoking the insatiability associated with all idolatry while presenting marriage as the culprit for our dissatisfaction. If only monogamy wasn't so stifling! If only marriage contained the spontaneity of a one-night stand! Are you discerning the antimarriage messages of culture, or are you believing the lies?

It is important to note that you don't need to have this all figured out! All of us are in *process* with every aspect of the Christian life, including our sexuality. But if there are unresolved sexual issues, do not continue putting it off. God wants to bring you to a place of peace. Because of Jesus, there is nothing to fear with bringing our sin and shame into the light. He promises to cover and cleanse us. He wants to remove the guilty stain from your experience because he longs for you to know the sweetness of his desire for you through the redemption of your sexuality.

Not "One Dreaded Conversation"

Hopefully you are convinced of the importance of giving your kids a robust picture of God's design for sex. Part of my hope in writing this book is to be a resource for parents who want to communicate more to their children than the basic mechanics and "Just wait until you're married!" There is so much more to be said. Given the cultural messages and mounting hormonal pressure, our kids need compelling reasons to obey God in their sexuality, especially as they approach their teen years and beyond. When it comes to talking to your kids about sex, getting out of your comfort zone means being willing to have multiple conversations with your kids.

If you have young children, start early! As soon as preschoolers start asking, "Where do babies come from?" they are ready for age-appropriate answers. The first thing we told our kids (when they were two or three years old) was that God makes a "special hug" for husbands and wives and that sometimes when they do that it makes a baby. For most kids that's enough. Although be forewarned, when one of my friends said this, her young children asked to watch! Don't let that prospect freak you out—it is just another opportunity to point to God's design, specifically the exclusive relationship that a married couple enjoys. Help them to see at the youngest age possible that marriage is a special relationship because it points to the unique, devoted relationship God wants to have with them.

It is crucial to start positive. God created sexuality to bring forth new life. He gave it as a gift to help bond a husband and wife. You can say sex is a special activity for married people to express their love and affection. Along these lines, you can make connections to other aspects of life they understand. Such as how much they enjoy snuggling on your lap or cuddling in bed. Or how nice it feels to receive a back rub or hug. You can compare to the ways you show affection to your child, while explaining that because marriage is a very special relationship, it is a unique form of affection. And the specialness of marriage is ultimately a picture of the special relationship Jesus wants to have with each one of us. You can describe how a husband and wife know everything about each other.

They experience all of life together. This is a snapshot of how Jesus is always with us, knows us perfectly, and experiences everything we experience because his Spirit lives inside of us.

As they get older, continue to answer their questions at an appropriate level. Our daughters were in early elementary school when they asked more specific questions about sexual mechanics. At that point, we talked about how God designed the penis and vagina to fit together. We shared how Mommy supplies the egg and Daddy supplies the sperm. I remember sketching this out on a napkin at the dinner table. Of course, it wasn't until much later that we gave them more specifics about orgasms and ejaculation, erections and vaginal lubrication.

The benefit of discussing sexuality at a young age is kids have no shame associated with it. Shame and embarrassment develop either through their own experience (with masturbation, pornography, or worse), or because parental silence and peer whispers create the sense of a scandalous taboo. My wife recounted hearing another child called a whore for the first time on the elementary school playground. She didn't know what it meant, but she knew from the hushed, venomous tone that something shocking had just occurred. She mentally filed it away (misspelled under H) as a really bad word, eventually learning it was connected in some way with this other thing you weren't supposed to talk about. This small example indicates how shame can be injected into a child's understanding of sexuality.

Far more tragic was my friend's invitation to come see what he found in the basement. Or the little girl across the street that initiated sexual play with me. It wasn't until much later that I realized these must have been *learned* behaviors for her, likely evidence of abuse in her life. Your willingness to engage young children with these conversations is a vital safeguard for them. They need words to attach to broken things in this world. They need help navigating appropriate boundaries with their bodies. This includes discussing who is allowed to change their diapers and making clear they have a say about their bodies. That means encouraging a high five to the Sunday school teacher who really wants a hug, if your child is uncomfortable. And he shouldn't be forced to sit on Great Aunt Gertrude's lap at Christmas if she feels like a stranger. Teaching them to take ownership of their bodies means respecting your children when they ask you to stop tickling, even if they laugh hysterically and beg you to resume seconds later.

As often as possible, have these conversations with your kids together as a couple. Develop a plan together, and prayerfully ask God to lead conversations as they happen and to help you not infuse the discussion with your own shame or embarrassment. You want to avoid making this a topic that is relegated to a special time with only the same-sex parent. Sexuality should be woven into the normal life of a Christian family, openly discussed as the topic arises. You should talk as freely about sexuality as discussing the news, politics, issues of faith, or the happenings of the school and workday.

As with every other aspect of your relationship, how you handle the issue of sexuality will change as your kids approach their teen years. There may be increased awkwardness as you discuss sexuality, especially if their sexual sin enters the picture. The most important thing about this stage is for you to begin to see your kids as emerging *adults*. It is the time for an arm-around-their-shoulder, side-by-side adult conversations, not for speaking down to them as children. This is also the season where conversations with the same-sex parent need to eclipse the family-wide discussions. In recent years it has been a little unsettling for me to be excluded as my biological daughters grow closer with their adopted mother, but I know this is appropriate and a real blessing from God given our unique family situation. Likewise, I anticipate the day when my young son and I will relate more deeply as men in a way that appropriately excludes my wife.

This means risking a greater level of vulnerability on your part. You can't read Proverbs 5–7 without getting a sense that the father, who's speaking to his son, understands the lure of temptation. Chapter 7 in particular uses such vivid detail, appealing to all the senses, depicting a scenario that would deeply entice any young man. It's clear the father "gets it," as he acknowledges the strong pull of sexual sin. But then he concludes with the stark warning: "All at once he follows her, as an ox goes to the slaughter" (v. 22). We must be clear about consequences, but honesty with our children includes not shrinking back from the reality that sin is incredibly alluring, even to us. If passing along our faith is the most important gift we give our kids, we must be willing to let them see how desperately we need Jesus every day. And that includes our need for his mercy and empowering grace to have sexual faithfulness.

At every stage of development there are issues to address with your kids, which is why you need to plan on multiple conversations over the years. If this sounds terrifying, remember God has promised to never leave you or forsake you. The Christian faith is learning to live with increasing dependence on him—trusting him with all our hearts and not leaning on our own understanding (see Proverbs 3:5). Jesus taught that we can never bear fruit on our own but, as we abide in him, our fruit will abound (see John 15:1–11). This is counterintuitive, but when you feel most overwhelmed you often are seeing with greater clarity. We weren't designed for self-sufficiency; we were designed for dependence on our Creator. Lean in to him with this. As you do, you will find he is able to do immeasurably more than you could ask or think (Ephesians 3:20). Keep that in mind as we consider the following sexual challenges facing our kids in the twenty-first century.

Our kids should be taught to be sexually obedient in order to faithfully follow Jesus, not because there will be a huge return on their sacrifice when they finally marry. This is another lie of the abstinence movement. God promises no one an amazing sex life. I've met so many Christians who entered marriage as virgins and have struggled sexually. If we give any motivation for chastity other than obedience to Christ, we are setting our kids up for failure, giving false motives for obedience, and failing to give them an accurate picture of the Christian life. We obey because "the love of Christ controls us" (2 Corinthians 5:14), not to make him our debtor for future blessings, as if he owes us for our obedience.

If your child is disabled, you will face unique challenges. Some disabled adults go on to marry, but for others this will be impossible. If there are cognitive challenges, you will need to discern the appropriate level of information. It is good to seek professional counsel, but you need to be wary. A good friend recounted seeking input on these matters and the prevailing "wisdom" was to allow the child to experience sex, no matter what. Some would advocate hiring prostitutes, rather than allow the child to die as a virgin. Obviously this reflects a culture that places a supreme value on sex and sees a sexless life as a tragedy. By God's grace, there is a richness to life in this world apart from sex. And my aforementioned friend would want you to know that whenever God takes something away from you, he *always* gives something back for the journey to sustain you, but you need to have eyes of faith to see this.

Masturbation

Despite how uncomfortable this may be for all involved, you must be willing to speak to your kids about the issue of masturbation. First, most parents are confronted with a child's exploration of his or her genitals at a young age. It is important to note that this is not masturbation. It is ordinary childhood exploration, and how you respond is crucial. You must never shame your child. As they get older you can talk about God creating our genitals for something special in marriage, opening the door to have positive discussions about God's design. Acknowledge that touching yourself is a nice feeling but that there is an appropriate context for this. Perhaps make the connection to eating dessert at specific times. You don't eat chocolate cake for breakfast because it's not the right time. Or maybe talk about Christmas gifts—you need to be patient and wait, leaving them under the tree until the right time. If you sneak down in the night and open your gifts, you'll still receive them eventually, but it will take away the delight of Christmas morning.

As your kids grow, you need to acknowledge the majority of teens wrestle with sexual desire and masturbation on some level. Are you willing to be vulnerable and discuss your own history with this issue? Will you encourage them to confide in you and offer your support in temptation? This is an invitation to a deeper level of intentional discipleship with your teens, calling them to a fuller understanding of what it means to be a follower of Jesus and pointing to how he wants to meet and strengthen them in their weakness (see 2 Corinthians 12:9–10).

This is also a time when teens need to learn that the Christian life requires *community*. There is no significant struggle that God wants us to face with him alone. There is a reason he places us in the body. The Song of Solomon beautifully expresses this reality as the third voice throughout the poems are the "Others," also referred to as the "daughters of Jerusalem." This underscores the importance of the community of faith coming alongside young lovers, evaluating, affirming, and blessing the potential union—or expressing concern if necessary.

Further, this is an opportunity for your teens to begin considering how they turn to false comforts to cope with the challenges of life in a fallen world. It is helpful for you to model repentance here. What false comforts tug at your heart when you are stressed? Acknowledge your own weakness and propensity to turn to the things of the world instead of God. Your honest self-disclosure invites them to pray for you in real ways and demonstrates your own ongoing need for Christ's mercy and the empowerment of his Spirit.

Help your kids learn to increasingly bring their pain to God, against our natural propensity toward false comforts. As discussed in chapter 8, the various psalms of lament provide a helpful framework to communicate the depth of our emotions while placing our hope in God. Using examples from your own life, pray through these psalms with your teen. Help them to learn how to communicate their fears, disappointments, and frustrations in a way that is honest but still honors God and trusts him. This is a central component to the life of faith: learning to wrestle with God. The profound angst of the teen years is a critical time for them take ownership of their faith by honestly dealing with their emotions before God.

Technology

The misuse of technology is often closely associated with masturbation, and the damaging nature of today's internet porn cannot be overstated. Any parent unwilling to guard technology is abdicating a significant parental role in the twenty-first century. Fortunately, there are many helpful tools to guard your home network and their devices. Loving your children means doing the research and taking the necessary steps. Neglecting this is like leaving hard-core pornography DVDs laying around your family room or inviting a pedophile to babysit your children.

Although the initial software and filters were pretty clunky, monitoring technology has vastly improved. The best devices are those linked directly to your router. Usually there is the ability to place varying levels of restriction on different devices, so that the home PC can be set at a very high level of search filtering to protect young children, while an older teen's smart phone might have no restrictions at all. But there is the capability of viewing the browser history on all devices.

Some of these products also have an "on the go" feature that maintains filtering and tracks the data usage of phones, iPads, etc, and even monitors the devices on other networks. In other words, your kids couldn't go to a friend's house, turn off their smartphone's data, log on to another network, and view porn. The restrictions you establish will remain enforced, as will the tracking of internet browsing. I am intentionally not promoting specific software because they are changing all the time. But do some research and determine what will work best for your family.

The most important thing is to take steps. Remember, the culture is eager to disciple your kids sexually, so do not shirk this essential aspect of twenty-first-century parenting. But you'll want to avoid two extremes: burying your head in the sand and feigning ignorance, or turning your home into a digital Fort Knox. The first thing to do is to talk to your kids. In an age-appropriate way, explain to them there are things online that they shouldn't see. For younger children, I describe it like seeing a scary TV commercial. As parents you try to shield them from things that will be harmful. Older kids need a franker discussion about the dangers of pornography that we discussed in the last chapter. And you should make clear that the whole family needs to be protected. Parents aren't immune to the seduction or destruction of porn. You are discussing it with them because you want them to know you are looking out for them and you want to be upfront with them about this. In this way you will model what it means to leave darkness behind and walk in the light.

As your kids are in their teen years, it makes sense to give them greater freedom, while continuing to monitor their access. They need to learn to make wise choices while they are under your roof, not be forced into a lockstep obedience they can gleefully cast off as soon as they are away from home. This means there will likely be missteps. These are opportunities to engage them with the comfort and call of the gospel. Of course, each child is an individual and requires a specific discipleship plan. If specific children demonstrate they struggle with porn, they may need greater restrictions, as well as greater attention from you in this regard.

The most basic level of parental oversight is accountability software and shared passwords. Your children should never have a device that you aren't free to pick up and access at any time. And they should know that you are paying attention to their internet history. Help them understand that accountability to you is a reflection of an infinitely greater cosmic reality. All of us are answerable to God. In our home, oversight includes sharing the same online purchasing account. All the apps our daughters download come on my phone as well. I have access to all the music they buy. A child struggling with porn requires greater oversight. For example, most of the men in my ministry have smartphones with significant restrictions. They are unable to download or delete apps. They have no internet access. Given their history with sexual sin, they need walls on tech that are stout and high. For your kids, use search engines to learn about parental controls for whatever type of phone or device they possess.

While enforcing appropriate boundaries, it is critical to call one another to honesty. Your kids should hear from you that all of us struggle with sin and you do not expect perfection, but you do expect they will confess when they fail. Help them see their integrity is vitally important in this struggle. Our hope in Jesus is that our sin is atoned for, so they are free to be exposed because he cleanses and covers (see 1 John 1:7–2:2). I urge you to demonstrate the importance of this by imposing greater discipline when they are caught in sin but show a measured mercy (this does not mean zero consequences) when they freely confess. Make it easy to come into the light!

Finally, start with the lowest level boundaries first and intensify only if they do not work. A kid who just received his first smartphone and confesses to viewing porn does not necessarily need to get smacked back down to a retro flip phone to match his grandmother's. It may come to that, but start small. Good discipline is not punitive because Jesus was punished for us. Discipline, though painful at times, is intended to steer us in the right direction (see Hebrews 12:5–13). Discipline, including establishing boundaries, should fit the circumstances. For example, when I started gardening I lived in a denser neighborhood. All I needed was low chicken wire to keep out the rabbits and groundhogs. Now, I live a few miles farther away from Philadelphia, and I'm battling deer. I have a seven-foot fence—and a shotgun on my Christmas list. Do not put restrictions on your child that equate to the seven-foot fence if you are only dealing with a rabbit-sized porn issue.

I do not take sin lightly or minimize the effects of pornography. (Reread the relevant section of the last chapter if you are unconvinced.) I am just zealous for you to wisely safeguard your relationship with your children and avoid exasperating them (as we are warned in Scripture; see Ephesians 6:4; Colossians 3:21). A severe Fort Knox approach will produce short-term compliance, but it is unlikely to form mature disciples of Christ. Only repentance and a deepening relationship with him will do that. Parent to those ends![1]

LGBTQ+ Issues

In twenty-first-century Western culture, we are confronted by a multitude of sexual identities that create significant challenges for Christian parents. Many of us have extended family members who've embraced an LGBTQ+ identity. Some of you are experiencing this with your own children. Others are shepherding their younger kids through friendships with children who have two same-sex parents. Older kids often have friends at school identifying as LGBTQ+, and this is happening more and more at earlier ages. We must acknowledge that times have changed and start facing these issues head-on.

For a long time, I thought I was empathizing with our daughters by saying, "I get it. High school wasn't *that* long ago. It *is* hard." When their school performed *Rent* a couple years ago, we got the film version from the library to watch as a family so they could get excited about the show, learn the music, and so on. Wow. My wife left to go to bed early. My daughters and I soldiered through to the bitter end. When it was over, I apologized. As Bob Dylan said, the times, they are a-changin'. Indeed. My high school would have never performed that show. My daughters' high school experience is profoundly different than mine. In a much humbler posture, I acknowledged, "Okay, I really don't know. Help me understand. Talk to me about your experience."[2]

You will need wisdom to know when to engage these issues. My first wife's uncle has been out of the closet for a long time. This meant that we talked to our daughters about homosexuality sooner than we would have preferred. But it made sense to have an intentional conversation together as a family, rather than risk an impromptu question during Christmas dinner about his unusual living arrangement with his partner. You may encounter a similar situation in your extended family, neighborhood, or school that will force your hand and necessitate this conversation. It is important to communicate that all of us are sinners in need of God's mercy. People involved in homosexuality are not on a different plane of wickedness. They are contending with a broken sexuality, just like the rest of us. These conversations should be marked by compassion, not self-righteous condemnation. By acknowledging recent examples of sin in your child's life (and your own), help them see that even those seeking to follow Jesus often fail. And those who do not know God usually live in ways very different from his design. As it says in Judges, when there is no king, everyone does what is right in their own eyes (see 17:6; 21:25). If it is hard for Christians to obey, how foreign is God's design for those who do not know him?

When facing these issues, remember the end of the story. The book of Revelation is not a complicated mystery. It is very simple. One of my seminary professors summed it up well. In the end, Jesus wins! Right now we are heralds of his coming kingdom. That's all. We do not need to win every argument and have the place of honor in the city square. We just need to be faithful witnesses for the true King. And, as it did for the apostles, bearing witness in our lives will likely mean enduring hardship and persecution while responding in love. This is the pattern left by Jesus: "If anyone would come after me, let him deny himself and take up his cross and follow me" (Matthew 16:24).

I am disheartened when Christians email me in outrage because their child's elementary school has an anti-bullying program seeking to protect "sexual minorities." Are you kidding me? Don't these people realize that Jesus *hates* bullying? Christians should be at the forefront of combating this sin. We should train our kids to befriend the downtrodden—including those identifying as LGBTQ+—and to stand between them and the bullies. Christians should be creating their own anti-bullying campaigns in every school because God hates injustice and abuse. This does not have to entail supporting sinful sexual behavior, but we must never lose sight of the larger issues of mercy and justice as we lament the lack of righteousness. I would love to see more Christian families willing to get outside their comfort zone and engage nontraditional families in genuine friendship.

As your kids approach their teen years, you must keep dialoguing about these issues. The younger generations are overwhelmingly embracing the LGBTQ+ narrative, having been powerfully influenced by the expressive individualism spirit of the age. The constant media onslaught and the personal stories of their peers are strong influences. You need to continue shoring up a biblical perspective of humanity's need for redemption and the original design of our good Creator God.

And encourage them (and the youth pastor!) to make their youth group a safe place! So many same-sex attracted teens have shared the pain of ridicule and rejection from their peers at church. Know the tragic reality that the gay community is excited to embrace with open arms any child from a Christian home who is struggling or confused about their sexuality or gender.

Finally, we need to speak honestly about the issues. Portraying a caricature of the gay community based on the extremes of pride-parade pictures is not telling the truth. The church has painted the gay community as only oversexed and promiscuous, not caring about relationships or fidelity. This is not a fair portrayal. It is like saying heterosexuality is typified by drunken, carousing college students on spring break. Now, I realize there are those in the gay community who do not care about marriage or fidelity. But the push to legalize gay marriage demonstrates that there are many gay couples who want to marry into monogamous, committed relationships. The point is that we need to be honest and not perpetuate a distorted image of the gay community. That is, we need to *obey Jesus* when he tells us to treat others as we want them to treat us (Matthew 7:12; Luke 6:31). As Christians, we do not want to be known in caricature as hateful bigots who want homosexuals to burn in hell. Telling the truth aligns us with the One who is truth incarnate. Dishonesty, or spinning truth, is counter to the kingdom of God. There is a significant practical concern here: if you are not honest with your kids and depict the gay community as having "horns and a tail," what will happen when your kids meet gay people and they do not fit your portrayal? It will call to question the veracity of everything else you have taught them. This is exactly where many millennials find themselves today, and they're leaving the church.

The Hookup Culture

When I began my college career in the late eighties, students of both genders competed to be the first in the dorm room to have sex. Accordingly, new student orientation involved randomly selected couples who were blindfolded and then raced to put a condom over a banana. But despite the decadence and prevalence of one-night stands, most sexual activity when I was in college still happened in relationships. They may not have lasted long, but there was more to it than just sex. HIV was still fairly new and terrifying, but I think it was more than that—there was still some awareness that sex *meant* something. It wasn't just a random, pleasurable recreation.

Recent decades have further eroded sexual mores. Now there are apps showing you who is available for sex within minutes of your current location. As mentioned in chapter 9, we are becoming more bestial, and our kids need help processing this, especially as their own hormones may be suggesting these apps are worth a try.

One of the biggest issues facing Christian kids is diminishing the behaviors labeled as sexual sin. From my experience with youth ministry, a perennial question of hormone-spiking teens was "How far is too far?" (Usually this question was asked on a late Saturday night during a retreat.) You get the picture of them wanting to inch their toes as close to the line as possible, and then lean in and hang their upper bodies over the line—while being careful not to lose their balance and fall headlong. The challenge is helping them to see that they're asking the wrong question! The only reason we should be looking for the boundary line in a dating relationship is to turn and run as fast as we can in the opposite direction.

As we've seen, sexual immorality in the Bible is any type of unchastity—basically any genital contact outside marriage. This is why Paul teaches, "But among you there must not be even a hint of sexual immorality" (Ephesians 5:3, NIV).

Clearly sexual immorality encompasses more than intercourse. In *God Loves Sex*, Allender and Longman encourage
greater levels of physical intimacy between unmarried couples based on their level of commitment, including "intimate
touching" outside of marriage. But this dismisses the stringent
biblical boundaries around sexual behavior and the exclusivity of genital contact reserved for marriage. Their arguments
are a response to today's culture, believing complete chastity
is "unrealistic and even absurd" given that "marriage tends
to be delayed till long after the point of sexual maturation."[3]
Given the text from Ephesians, it is hard to conceive the apostle Paul making these concessions. One of the standard Old
Testament formulas for immorality is "uncovering" another's nakedness. The Bible consistently upholds there is only
one relationship where we are invited to be naked without
shame—and that is always on the heels of making lifelong,
covenantal promises.

Further, our kids need to understand the integration of
our body and spirit. The physiological processes God built
into the system are to reinforce marital bonding. This means
there is a one-flesh experience when we have sex. In particular,
I'm referring to the way our *feelings* bind two people together
through sexual activity. This is, after all, how God intended
it to work. The problem is creating a sense of bonding where
no meaningful bond exists. This sense of bonding happens
whenever and however we experience the physiological rush
of sexual connection.

Outside of marriage this deep sense of connection creates
confusion. I challenge young adults that choosing a spouse is
the most important decision of their life! They wouldn't drink
three beers before taking the GRE because they want to be
thinking as clearly as possible during the exam. Similarly, in a
dating relationship, the experience of bonding through sexual
release brings a dense fog and prevents clarity. This means you
might miss red flags that would be obvious if sober-minded,

or you might lose the ability to hear from others who see the warning signs. Scripture exhorts us, "Brothers, do not be children in your thinking. Be infants in evil, but in your thinking be mature" (1 Corinthians 14:20). Only through obedience will we be clearheaded.

Many kids from Christian homes will not go completely crazy. The hookup culture will most likely influence them by watering down the Bible's sexual ethic. Christian singles justify crossing lines in their dating relationships because everybody else is doing so much worse, including some of their Christian friends. In my experience, the majority of single Christians in their twenties are sexually active on some level in their dating relationships. My friends who pastor millennials say it is incredibly common to learn that members of their church are living together unmarried and see no inconsistency with having sex on Saturday night and partaking of the Lord's Supper on Sunday morning. They may not be using hookup apps, but the hookup culture has deep hooks in the next generation of the body of Christ.

The Most Important Sex Ed

Your marriage is the most important sex education you give your children. Often teens look at their parents' relationship and conclude, "Are you kidding me? Wait for that?! I'm going to enjoy life while I can!" We need to do the hard work of cultivating deep, passionate marital intimacy to demonstrate that marriage is worth waiting for. Our lives will always speak far louder than our words. And when our teens are wrestling with the considerable challenge of raging hormones, our words will carry little weight if they do not see the fruit of a good marriage borne out in our lives. We need to demonstrate that marriage is worth waiting for.

Does your marriage reflect the lies of this world that marriage kills good sex? Or does it demonstrate that the kingdom has come and Jesus is making all things new? I have seen him enable passion and intimacy to flourish even decades into marriage. This does not mean trying to baptize the world's obsession, turning every night into an endless quest for greater pleasure. Rather, it means realizing that marital intimacy matters and working to cultivate this in your marriage, including the deeper *yada* that enriches sexuality.

Marriage is hard. All of us have sinned against our spouse in front of our kids. But it is never too late to turn things around. If you are facing significant problems, seek help. Talk to your pastor or ask for a referral for an experienced Christian counselor. If you have a spouse who is unwilling to seek help, go alone. Even if just one of you is open to examining your heart and begins doing a different dance, it will change the dynamic in your relationship. Generally, we need the wise perspective from someone outside our family who can see the pitfalls and point us to paths of healing. If you aren't connected to a church or you exist on the periphery of church life, commit to seeking God in community and building real relationships with others. It's an oxymoron and completely foreign to the New Testament to try to live the Christian life without community. Again, commit to seeking this fellowship even if your spouse is currently uninterested.[4] This could be an incredible discipleship opportunity—as God changes your marriage, your kids will see the power of the gospel at work in your home. There is nothing more potent than this to show them the truth of the hope we have.

The Challenge of Single Parenting

While working on this project, a close friend lost his dear wife. I have ached for him and his children, knowing the brutal pain of this season. If you know single parents, invite the family over for dinner. Call them on the weekends and invite them to do activities. It seems like single parents are often forgotten by other families in the church.

If you are the single parent, then it's critical for you to solicit help from the broader church. Prayerfully consider who can assist you in this process. Do you have wise members of your extended family? Are you a part of a home Bible study or have close Christian friends who can come alongside you? A good friend recounted that he learned about sexuality through his mom's long-term boyfriend. It was a little awkward, but he remembered that the man was direct, honest, and not embarrassed. This is not a best case, single-parent scenario, but it is a picture of a single mom trying to do right by her son and realizing he needed a man to speak to him about these issues in ways she was unable.

Although sexuality was very openly discussed in our home since my daughters were young, when my first wife died, I was incredibly blessed to have other women step in and care for them in areas I couldn't help as a man. I did go first-time bra shopping with my daughters as a single dad (quite the surreal experience), but I couldn't really instruct on the proper use of menstrual pads. (And let me warn you right now: electric razors are NOT good for armpit hair!)

This underscores the necessity of being rooted in the body of Christ. At a time when society is increasingly fractured, the importance of having a strong community of faith is more critical than ever, and it is a powerful witness to a watching world. If you are a single parent, will you humble yourself and ask for help? There are probably so many areas you could benefit from getting assistance, but you need to reach out and let people know. Until people have walked through it, they don't really get it; let others know so they can help you.

CHAPTER 12

Biblical Sexuality in Public

The Bible's restraint of sexual expression is one of the most significant stumbling blocks for those exploring Christianity. The stringent boundaries around human sexuality are a hard sell. But, for a long time, the biblical sexual ethic was the dominant ethic of American culture. Although there were always small subcultures going against the flow, these tended to be on the fringes of society—the bohemians living in Greenwich Village or the hippies in San Francisco. Even after the sexual and cultural revolution of the sixties and seventies, the majority of American society believed that sex was reserved for marriage, and behaviors like premarital cohabitation were generally frowned upon. But the last few decades have marked a dramatic shift toward a sexuality that wildly diverges from Christian orthodoxy. Many older folks have experienced moral whiplash with the dramatic changes in recent generations. The sexual ethic once taken for granted is seen as oppressive and harmful to society, and people who uphold biblical morality are going against the flow, often ridiculed as quaint and regressive.

The Supreme Court decision in 2015 that rendered same-sex marriage legal nationwide has led to a deepening societal perception that anyone who labels homosexuality as "sin" is a hater. Often when unbelievers learn of our faith, one of their first questions is "So, are you against gays?" When issues of faith are discussed with those outside the church, the church's traditional stance on same-sex marriage inevitably comes up, and this topic is hard to navigate.

With such an onslaught of negative press in the media and pop culture, not to mention pressure from friends and family, many Christians are struggling to stand for the truth. As the cultural battle for "marriage equality" began to build steam, there was a lot of inflammatory rhetoric. The term itself suggests those in opposition favor *inequality*. "I'm on the side of love" became the rallying cry, with the clear implication that any opposed were unloving. The signs after the decision underscored this with the declaration "Love Wins!"

All of this pressure can make it look really attractive to just give up and go with the flow. The world is constantly trying to cram us into its mold, and when it comes to sexual ethics, we are facing at least two significant challenges. First, there is the incredible social pressure described above and the challenge of being labeled intolerant, a grave offense in our culture. Second, all of us are wrestling with our own sexuality. This should help us to be compassionate toward others, but it also might tempt us to give ground on our beliefs since we are similarly tempted. I debated a pro-gay theologian years ago who said I had no right to call homosexuality a sin, basing his argument on Jesus's statement, "Let him who is without sin among you be the first to throw a stone at her" (John 8:7). I tried to gently show him that the point of that narrative is not that adultery does not matter because everyone sins but that everyone needs to repent. (When I preached on this passage years ago, I titled my sermon, "Everybody Should Get Stoned.") The perfect ending to the scene in this passage would have been all of the Pharisees on their knees in repentance, instead of them merely dropping their stones and slinking away.

In order to engage people in our lives outside the church, we need to understand their sexual worldview. We need to grasp the post-Christian script of contemporary American culture. There is a great precedent for this in Acts when Paul addressed the Greek philosophers: "Men of Athens, I perceive that in every way you are very religious. For as I passed along and observed the objects of your worship, I found also an altar with this inscription: 'To the unknown god.' What therefore you worship as unknown, this I proclaim to you" (Acts 17:22–23). He goes on to describe the one, true God, even incorporating lines from their poets (17:27–31). When we understand how others believe and think—going beyond straw man arguments—we will engage our culture in a way that woos them to Jesus and the hope we have in him.

My goal for this chapter is to help you facilitate discussions with unbelieving neighbors, coworkers, friends, and extended family. It is important to have a few foundational principles in place. First, Scripture assumes that your life will be salt and light to a dark and dying world. Consider this passage as it describes our interactions with unbelievers, "Have no fear of them, nor be troubled, but in your hearts honor Christ the Lord as holy, always being prepared to make a defense to anyone who asks you for a reason for the hope that is in you; yet do it with gentleness and respect" (1 Peter 3:14–15). There is an expectation that those around you will see a life that looks different, specifically a life characterized by *hope*. Hope is desperately needed in a fallen world, and it's in short supply. Madison Avenue offers hope—every new product is going to change your life. Politicians offer hope, declaring, "My platform focuses on your needs and will make your life better." Entertainment offers hope, inferring that this movie is going to be unlike anything you've seen before. In contrast to the smoke and mirrors offered by the culture, biblical hope is built on the rock-solid promises of God, which are rooted in his faithful acts of redemption.

Further, we are called to: "Walk in wisdom toward outsiders, making the best use of the time. Let your speech always be gracious, seasoned with salt, so that you may know how you ought to answer each person" (Colossians 4:5–6). We are told, "Show perfect courtesy toward all people, for we ourselves were once foolish, disobedient, led astray, slaves to various passions and pleasures" (Titus 3:2–3). This is critically important! Paul exhorts us to be courteous, saying, "Remember where *you* came from. Remember that you have been shown mercy and you desperately needed it." The only way we can show perfect courtesy and have gracious, salty words is if we are daily aware of our own need for God's grace. Most of us don't need to go beyond our own sexuality to see our need for grace. There's plenty of brokenness to go around.

This means we need to rediscover the ability to disagree with civility. One of the reasons I am disengaged from social media is that it seems to be seriously undermining our ability to discuss areas of difference. People lob grenades back-and-forth across cyberspace from behind the safety of their screens. Rather than really hearing one another and seeking to understand, people just attack. After Justice Antonin Scalia's passing, I was amazed and encouraged to hear stories about the warm friendship he enjoyed with Ruth Bader Ginsburg. How could this be?! You couldn't find two more ideologically opposed members of the Supreme Court! Yet there were reports of their friendship—sharing meals and having genuine care *and respect* for each other. If those two could do it, the church of Jesus Christ, empowered by his Spirit, should be able to lovingly communicate with people who have widely divergent worldviews.

Communicating Christian Hope

A number of years ago I saw a brief video online of a secular reporter interviewing a well-known pastor on the issue of homosexuality. The pastor had only a couple minutes to respond. The essence of his argument was "I am an evangelical pastor who believes the Bible is God's Word. The Bible says homosexuality is wrong, so . . ." He literally shrugged his shoulders as if to communicate, "I'm sorry, I don't know what else to tell you." It was hard to watch because there is so much more to say.

First, we need to be willing to acknowledge that Christian sexual ethics go against the grain of our culture. I'd argue that we need the Holy Spirit not only to live out a biblical sexual ethic but even to agree that it is good. For example, before I came to faith, it made perfect sense to live with someone before marriage. This seemed like wisdom. After all, you don't *really* know someone until you live with them, right? Why would any sane person enter a lifelong relationship without having as much knowledge as possible? There seems to be truth in this worldly wisdom, unless you are illuminated by the Spirit and understand the wonder of God's design. This means acknowledging that it does not make much sense if you are not on the inside of the Christian faith. This frees you from operating under the mistaken belief that unbelievers are going to accept the truth of the gospel without converting in the process. In terms of representing the Christian ethic publicly, we should be trying to help outsiders understand why our beliefs lead to our sexual ethics. Of course, we pray that the Holy Spirit will show them the beauty and wisdom of God's design, but we know that this is a work of supernatural grace!

Today Christians must accept the return to our roots as a cultural minority, not the dominant voice and influence. But be encouraged—you have the opportunity to boldly herald the King prior to his return with the confidence that every knee will bow (Philippians 2:9–11). And church history reveals that some of the Spirit's most dynamic activity occurs when God's people are marginalized and even persecuted.

We also need to help people understand the big picture of what Christians believe. Take the conversation beyond the Bible's restrictions on sex and explain a Christian worldview. For example, you could say:

We believe that in the beginning God created everything and declared it to be very good. (I'd personally put the specifics of creation aside for the moment.) He had a purpose for his creation, especially for humanity. We were created to live in a relationship with him, serving as his representatives and stewards of the world, working to display his glory in the beautiful world he made. The goal of creation was for humanity to rule over and steward the earth as God's agents, so that eventually the glory of God would cover the earth as the waters cover the sea.

But then humanity turned against God, determined to live independently from him, and the ripple effects of that rebellion led to disorder in the world. Now everything is out of joint. The Bible describes this as all of creation groaning. As humanity turned away from God, we've turned on one another. Now it is instinctive from our earliest years to be selfish and fight for what we want. None of my children observed hitting or pushing and shoving in my home, but they began to do it instinctively. And what we see in the microcosm of our homes is played out globally as whole nations favor self over others, leading to oppression and injustice. But, if we are honest, the brokenness we see on the six o'clock news happens in our own hearts. And this disordering means that our natural inclinations are broken, including our sexuality. All of us are born with a sexuality that does not fit God's pattern.

Because God loves his creation, and humanity in particular, he established a plan for redemption and promised a Deliverer. He would personally enter the brokenness, identifying with his creation and suffering under the curse. He would willingly pay the price of death in order for reconciliation to happen. Forgiveness always costs. If you steal one thousand dollars from me and are absolutely unable to repay it, when I forgive you, I am out a thousand dollars. I need to absorb the cost. The same is true for God. He warned that rebellion would lead to death and estrangement. So when the people rebelled, he needed to endure death and estrangement in order for forgiveness to happen.

But this enabled humanity to be reconciled. Even better, Jesus poured out his Spirit who empowers obedience and establishes our constant relational bond with the Father and Son. Jesus is gathering people from every tongue, tribe, and nation to serve him and work together to bring his kingdom to this hurting world, while we wait for his return and the re-creation of the cosmos.

To understand the Christian view of sexuality, you need to understand we view the world through these phases of creation, fall, redemption, and eventual glorification. Christians feel strongly about sex because we believe God built our sexuality into creation for specific reasons. One obvious reason is to produce offspring. This reflects who he is as the Creator of life. Further, the Bible describes marriage as a picture of Christ and his church. This is why Christians believe that sex is limited to a lifelong, exclusive relationship. It is a picture in this life of our spiritual fidelity to God. We believe gay marriage violates the design on two counts: it does not have the potential to produce life, and it does not reflect the unity and diversity of heterosexual union that points to Christ and the church.

Of course, this is a very detailed schematic overview of how to explain a Christian view of sex to outsiders. Every actual conversation needs to take into account the specific situation in which it occurs and the relationship. But wherever and whenever we speak publicly about our sexual ethic, we need to help a confused world understand that it is part of a holistic view of life in the kingdom of God.

Pursue Relationship

If we take seriously the call to be salt and light, it means engaging nontraditional families in relationship. We must risk the awkwardness of certain conversations, especially if kids are involved. We need to get outside our comfort zone to pursue people very different than us. But consider—doing this looks like Jesus! He set his glory aside, leaving the infinite wonders of heaven to come suffer under the curse. He didn't shrink back from difficult circumstances but pursued us. This means he knows how to help you when you invite the gay couple and their child over for dinner.

Rosaria Butterfield was an English professor at Syracuse University, specializing in queer theory, when she wrote a scathing op-ed piece on Promise Keepers, a Christian men's movement. She received hundreds of letters, both hate and fan mail. And she received one letter from a local pastor that she wasn't quite sure how to categorize. Clearly he wasn't a fan, but it wasn't full of hate. He asked a lot of questions and invited her to a meal at his home with him and his wife. She recounts how their pursuit of her in genuine friendship was used by God to begin wooing her to himself.[1] It may not feel this way, but "the fields are white for harvest" (John 4:35) in post-Christian America.

Here are some thoughts about building relationships with LGBTQ+ people in your life. First, don't feel like you need to call them out on their sin. Although we are willing to overlook all kinds of sin in unbelievers, for some reason with the gay community we feel the need to make sure they know we regard what happens in their bedroom as sin. If you're in line at the grocery store and the guy behind you is on the phone cursing up a storm, I am sure you don't ask him to stop. Hopefully, you pray for him, but you don't confront him. It wouldn't be appropriate—you don't even know his name! Similarly, if your neighbor has a drinking problem, you probably wouldn't call her out, unless she asks, "My husband says I drink too much. What do you think?" A wise person would probably ask her some follow-up questions to understand more of the context, but then it'd be loving to express your concern. Let her know what you've observed, that you've been praying for her, and that you'd like to assist her in getting help. The point is you need a relationship to have these conversations and be invited to speak.

The same is true with your gay friends. If they know you are a Christian, they probably assume you think homosexuality is wrong. I suspect eventually they'll ask you. When they do, be ready to prayerfully answer. But your first move in the relationship shouldn't be calling them out on their sin. Consider this helpful teaching from 1 Corinthians 5:9–10: "I wrote to you in my letter not to associate with sexually immoral people—not at all meaning the sexually immoral of this world, or the greedy and swindlers, or idolaters, since then you would need to go out of the world." This is so important for us as Christians. We are not called by the New Testament to impose our sexual ethics on others—they are hard enough for us to live out with the Holy Spirit. We are called to be salt and light to people with radically contrary lives and worldviews so that the glory of Jesus is evident to a watching world.

One of the things that amazed Rosaria about her pastor friend is that he confessed his own sin in prayer in front of her. He modeled repentance and demonstrated a genuine relationship with God. She was drawn to his intimacy with God, not immediately convicted because her life was sinful. They had in-depth discussions about the Bible and theology, sexual ethics and politics, but it was in the context of mutual respect, not self-righteous condemnation. Our calling is to manifest the love of God in Christ. If we are asked about the truth of biblical ethics, we should answer without hesitation or equivocation. But the key is keeping in step with the Spirit, entrusting the timing of these conversations to him. I suspect those most eager to speak truth will need to learn greater patience as they first pray and listen, while those who might shrink back from confrontation need to ask for boldness and be ready when the time comes.

Rosaria recounts that the pastor and his wife didn't initially share the gospel or invite her to church. They didn't make her feel like the recipient of a tiny evangelistic crusade. Instead, they demonstrated genuine interest in her personally, her relationships (including her lesbian partner), and her work. It is so important to truly befriend people, not take on projects. People can tell whether you genuinely care for them or if you're just trying to get another jewel for your crown.

I want you to know this is possible! Previously, I had a next-door neighbor who was a lesbian. She knew I was a conservative pastor and asked no more questions. We had a casual friendship. My first wife went out for coffee with her a couple of times. When Sandy passed, I told my neighbor the exact nature of my ministry. I didn't want her to come to the memorial service, hear about Harvest USA, and look it up on her own. She was gracious, and it actually opened a door for more honest conversation. She shared about coming to the realization that she was a lesbian, and she opened up about other personal issues in her life. We shared meals that eventually included her partner. She observed the girls and me through our loss and my years of single parenting. On one occasion, she was gardening on the side of her house, unbeknownst to me, while I talked with one of my daughters on the front porch. When we chatted a couple days later, she mentioned overhearing the conversation and confided, "Your daughters are having a very different experience of a father than I had." The day we moved away, she came out of her house in tears, hugging us and telling us how much she would miss us! She has since moved out of state, and we've lost touch, but I continue to pray for her, hopeful that God will woo her to himself.

My point is not to toot my own horn. I want to encourage you that if God can give me a friendship with someone who knows that my ministry stands in opposition to her way of life, he has grace for you in whatever relational situations he may land you! I hope you will catch a vision for how exciting it could be for your family to have a robust faith in Christ's kingdom going forward. I hope that, rather than shrinking back from hard situations, you will plunge in because you believe that the Spirit of Jesus goes before you. Our children need to see the power of the gospel at work. Your trust in God's grace to cross these cultural divides as heralds of his kingdom is a beautiful place to start.

CHAPTER 13

Sex and Eternal Hope

We are in the time of Advent as I complete this writing. This is often a very hard season, all the more because it's supposed to be "the most wonderful time of the year." Far from alleviating pain, the holidays seem to shine a bright light on everything that is off-kilter—displaying brokenness in sharp relief. Absence due to estranged relationships is more acute. The messaging and expectations of a materialist culture make us feel diminished because the packages under the tree and the spread on the table seem sparse. In grief, we are aware of empty seats, even if the table is full.

Genuine, biblical Christianity is honest about the pain. Advent is about aching for Christ's return as much as it celebrates Jesus's birth. (Think of carols like "O Come, O Come Emmanuel" or "Come Thou Long Expected Jesus.") Why? Because despite the Cross, Resurrection, Ascension, and outpouring of the Spirit, this world is woefully broken. We continue to suffer under the curse, and death and disease seem to get the last word. And so we await the final deliverance when Jesus returns to set all things right.

Some of you feel this poignantly in your sexuality, especially because our culture has convinced you that sex is the pinnacle of human experience. Perhaps lifelong, faithful singleness has left you with unanswered questions, along with unsatisfied yearning. Or maybe a past season of sexual activity means you've tasted the pleasure and that memory seems to intensify the absence. Others are disillusioned in marriage. I have met so many Christians whose sexual experience pales in comparison to their expectations. After one older brother was diagnosed with prostate cancer he compared his sex life to owning a beach house. "I've visited a few times in my life. I've seen pictures of a lot of other people having fun there. And now I've just received notice that the house is getting torn down." This echoes the disappointment of so many who longed for a rich sex life only to have their hopes swept out to sea. Whether you have been single your entire adult life, are single again, or are in a marriage that is deeply broken, God wants to meet you in your places of pain. He is the "God of all comfort, who comforts us in all our afflictions" (2 Corinthians 1:3–4). He wants to satisfy your soul in ways that sex *never* will.

Because our sexuality reflects the transcendence of our relationship with God, even those with a rich, satisfying sexual relationship feel this ache of longing. In all of life's pleasures, we get only brief glimpses of glory that quickly vanish. Even at its glorious best, sex is just a signpost pointing beyond itself to the Giver of this wondrous gift. Sex is like seeing the Rocky Mountains in an IMAX theater. It might be an amazing, breathtaking display. But it's still just a two-dimensional experience. The promise of our future is that one day we'll be hiking, skiing, and mountain biking on those heights!

Just a Signpost

There is a reason why sexual behavior and the allure of romance are such powerful idols. They provide an experience that is *otherworldly*. This amazing signpost points to the new heavens and new earth that is fast approaching. But the temptation is to be mesmerized by the signpost rather than do the hard work of journeying over rough, rocky ground through the torrential downpours and alternating seasons of biting cold and scorching heat. Sometimes we walk a long way through excruciating conditions before we come to another signpost. This makes it really tempting to just sit and stare at the signpost. One purpose of this life is growing in our trust and love for God, learning that he is truly present and faithful as we go through the suffering and trials, walking mile after painful mile and holding onto the hope that we are not abandoned. At the beginning, perhaps you had only the vaguest sense that Someone was there. As the long miles stretch out behind you, there can be a growing awareness that, indeed, there *is* Someone beside you. But to experience this, you must gird up your loins and face the times of traveling through the vast wilderness between signposts, while holding on to the promises.

Of course, sex is just one of God's signposts. Despite the fall, this is a beautiful world, filled with blessings in which God pours out his goodness on all creation—"For he makes his sun rise on the evil and on the good, and sends rain on the just and on the unjust" (Matthew 5:45). We need our eyes open wide to all the signposts. Praise him as you sit before a crackling fire on a winter night. Know his smile as you laugh with friends. Rejoice as you savor food and drink. Hear his wooing in all your experiences of pleasure.

But wherever we are, we need to see Jesus more clearly at the signpost of sex. Are you allowing the blessings you experience to deepen your love for the Giver of all good gifts? Does your pleasure in marriage (sexual and otherwise) lead to worship? Are you able to give thanks in your singleness and allow your longings and sexual desires to direct you to his heart for you? Can you hold fast to his promises to make your life fruitful for his kingdom even in the absence of marriage or biological children? This is the call of the Christian to go deeper with him through the pilgrimage of life in this world in preparation of the world to come.

A Lifelong Engagement

Throughout the Bible, God expresses his connection to his people in almost every conceivable human relationship: king/subject, master/servant, father/child, older brother/younger sibling, friend/friend. As we've seen, the most astounding is God's use of the marriage metaphor, wherein Jesus has the role of the Bridegroom. All of us should want to experience the full implication of this unbelievable statement, "'Therefore a man shall leave his father and mother and hold fast to his wife, and the two shall become one flesh.' This mystery is profound, and I am saying that it refers to Christ and the church" (Ephesians 5:31–32). He invites all of us—single and married—to a depth of personal intimacy with himself that the union of marriage is intended to symbolize.

This means all of our romantic longings point us to Jesus, the lover of our souls. He is an excited, husband-to-be who's looking forward to his wedding day. He is longing for the ultimate consummation of our union with him. Consider his words at the Last Supper: "I have earnestly desired to eat this Passover with you before I suffer. For I tell you I will not eat it until it is fulfilled in the kingdom of God" (Luke 22:15–16). Matthew and Mark also recount this statement of Jesus—but did you catch the exuberance in Luke's account? The phrase "earnestly desired" is translated in the King James Version as "with desire I have desired." Though it sounds awkward, this translation is much closer to the Greek. Jesus used both the noun and the verb forms for a phrase best rendered as a "strong desire." We talked about this Greek word, *epithumia*, previously because it is usually used to depict sexual desire and is typically translated "lust." In the strongest possible terms, Jesus expresses his longing to partake in the Passover with his disciples because it is a foretaste of the great wedding banquet that is coming.

I usually recommend short engagements for couples. After all, when you know you have found the one, there is no sense dancing around the fire waiting for a misstep. But the reality is the Christian experience is like a lifelong engagement. Our brief season in this world is about preparing for the life to come. We do that by deepening the intimacy with our Bridegroom, forsaking other lovers and drawing closer to him until we burn with desire in the hope of his return.

The Great Wedding Feast

All of human history is hurtling forward to a glorious consummation—the marriage supper of the Lamb:

> Then I heard what seemed to be the voice of a great multitude, like the roar of many waters and like the sound of mighty peals of thunder, crying out,
>> "Hallelujah!
>> For the Lord our God
>>   the Almighty reigns.
>> Let us rejoice and exult
>>   and give him the glory,
>> for the marriage of the Lamb has come,
>>   and his Bride has made herself ready;
>> it was granted her to clothe herself
>>   with fine linen, bright and pure"—
> for the fine linen is the righteous deeds of the saints. And the angel said to me, "Write this: Blessed are those who are invited to the marriage supper of the Lamb." And he said to me, "These are the true words of God." (Revelation 19:6–9)

Although pretty sparse in its description, this passage invites us to ponder the wonder of the new heavens and new earth. The Bible teaches us to expect "what no eye has seen, nor ear heard, nor the heart of man imagined, what God has prepared for those who love him" (1 Corinthians 2:9). But at the same time God gives us glimpses of the future that are stunning! When a man and woman enter marriage, they are overjoyed! They can't wait to be united, to become one flesh. Jesus is saying this delight is a snapshot of the longing in his heart. All human history is hurtling toward this day, anticipated by our Creator from eternity past. In Jesus, the God-man, heaven and earth are at last united. This is how Paul describes the beginning of our engagement period, "For in him all the fullness of God was pleased to dwell, and through him to reconcile to himself all things, whether on earth or in heaven, making peace by the blood of his cross" (Colossians 1:19–20). Paul goes on to describe the purpose of the Incarnation and our atonement as "making known to us the mystery of his will, according to his purpose, which he set forth in Christ as a plan for the fullness of time, to unite all things in him, things in heaven and things on earth" (Ephesians 1:9–10). Since his work of redemption, Jesus has eagerly looked forward to the consummation *with you!* He can't wait for you to see him face-to-face and begin eternity together.

Because he is the ultimate Bridegroom, Jesus taught there is no human marriage in heaven (see Matthew 22:23–33; Mark 12:18–27; Luke 20:27–40). He was challenged by the Sadducees about the reality of the resurrection with a mocking tale about a woman who married a man with six brothers, marrying each in succession after the previous one died. This story reflected a command from the Old Testament in which relatives were required to marry a widow and raise up an heir to perpetuate the name of the deceased (see Deuteronomy 25:5–10). Jesus responds to their mockery with a stinging rebuke: "You are wrong, because you know neither the Scriptures nor the power of God. For in the resurrection they neither marry nor are given in marriage, but are like angels in heaven" (Matthew 22:29–30). What is he saying? Human marriage is a phenomenon of this world intended to give a glimpse (as in a mirror darkly) of a future beyond our ability to comprehend. The momentary marriage of this world will be infinitely transcended in the world to come.

This means the sweetest moments of earthly marriage, whether the delights of sexual intimacy or the quiet joys of deep emotional connection, are only faint glimpses of the glories to come when we are fully united to Jesus. Sexuality and marriage are signposts to his infinitely greater love, commitment, delight, and pleasure in us. He is a God of pleasure, and his intention is to bless us. That's why the psalmist declares, "My soul will be satisfied as with fat and rich food" (63:5). We live in a culture that is sexually insane, desperate to find satisfaction and contentment that constantly elude us. Our culture is more prosperous and at ease than any other in the history of the world, but most of us are deeply discontent. God's promise is to satisfy our hungry souls. He promises that at his right hand are pleasures forevermore. He invites us to drink from his river of delights and feast on the abundance of his house. Even if you are not struggling significantly with sexual issues, I know that you know what it's like to live discontent. We use all kinds of things to try to find joy and contentment. For some it is sex or emotionally entangled relationships, while others strive for success, money, or material possessions. Anything our hearts turn to as a replacement for God leaves us empty and desolate.

Why do our desires feel so insatiable? Because they can be satisfied only by an infinite God. I love Paul's prayer that the Ephesians would "know the love of Christ that surpasses knowledge, that [they] may be filled with all the fullness of God" (Ephesians 3:19). What does that fullness look like? In Ephesians 4, Paul describes Jesus ascending to heaven to fill the entire universe (vv. 8–10). In a world clamoring with discontent, God promises to fill you with his infiniteness that fills the entire universe. In calling us to sexual fidelity, he is not taking something away from you. He is offering you a greater, richer life because he offers you himself! The Bible tells us we

can't begin to grasp the joy awaiting. The imagery of the resurrected Christ in Revelation 1:12–19 is so overwhelming that
John recounts falling at his feet like a dead man. But what does
Jesus do? This tender Bridegroom reaches out with his right
hand saying, "Fear not . . ." (v. 17).

Flesh and Spirit Forever

We've considered how the split between the physical and
spiritual is the result of secular philosophy and at odds with
the teaching of the Bible. This is most evident in Scripture's
teaching that our eternity will be not a disembodied spiritual
existence but a re-created cosmos. The Bible has always held
together the union of physical and spiritual as good creations
of God. Although spirit and flesh are often at war with each
other in this world (Galatians 5:17), the new heavens and new
earth will be the perfect harmony of heaven and earth and
of flesh and spirit. This is why Colossians 1 and Ephesians
1 express that both the physical and spiritual are united in
Jesus. Thus the Gospels record Jesus in his resurrection body
breaking bread, cooking fish on the beach, eating food, and
being touched by his followers. He is present and absolutely
solid. He tells his doubting disciples, "See my hands and my
feet, that it is I myself. Touch me, and see. For a spirit does
not have flesh and bones as you see that I have" (Luke 24:39).
At the same time, his physicality was radically changed. He
could disguise his appearance, pass through locked doors,
disappear in a flash and reappear miles away, and fly up into
the heavens. These are not examples of being purely *spiritual*
postresurrection, but rather he is now the "beginning, the
firstborn from the dead" (Colossians 1:18). His transformed
physicality is the beginning of the renewal eventually coming
to the entire cosmos.

C. S. Lewis's book *The Great Divorce* masterfully envisions what this could be like. Far from being a wispy, spiritual

existence, Lewis envisions the new creation as *more solid* than our current earth. The humans who have the opportunity to take a bus trip from the edge of hell to the outskirts of heaven are like wraiths. Semitransparent, they are too weak to even bend the grass. They walk on pinpricks as the blades of grass stab into the soles of their unsubstantial feet. Although purely speculative, think about it like this: Jesus is able to walk through locked doors not because he is insubstantial, but because he is so solid that he passes through doors like walking through water. The molecules of earthly objects shift like liquid around his infinitely more solid, resurrection body. We should understand our future hope to be a perfection of all that is good in the present life, not a denial of it.

The idea of the union between heaven and earth is beautifully depicted with the description of the new Jerusalem in Revelation:

> Then I saw a new heaven and a new earth, for the first heaven and the first earth had passed away, and the sea was no more. And I saw the holy city, new Jerusalem, coming down out of heaven from God, prepared as a bride adorned for her husband. And I heard a loud voice from the throne saying, "Behold, the dwelling place of God is with man. He will dwell with them, and they will be his people, and God himself will be with them as their God. He will wipe away every tear from their eyes, and death shall be no more, neither shall there be mourning, nor crying, nor pain anymore, for the former things have passed away." (Revelation 21:1–4)

Notice the holy city comes down from heaven to earth, uniting the two. This depicts the perfect union of the physical and spiritual, heaven and earth. Using similar wedding imagery, the city is like a bride prepared for her husband. And the ultimate union is expressed as we are promised that God himself will dwell with his people. Revelation 22 describes the river of life flowing from God's throne through the city, with the tree of life growing on both sides bearing fruit each month of the year, and then gives this moving phrase: "The leaves of the tree were for the healing of the nations" (v. 2). The brokenness will be undone. Everything sad will become untrue.

Although it is clear that these portrayals are to inspire our imagination of things that we can't begin to conceive, all of them depict a very physical world and an ongoing physical existence. Think about the descriptions of Jesus's resurrection body recounted earlier in this chapter. Scripture promises the body in store for you will be like Jesus's resurrection body (see Philippians 3:20–21). Compare an acorn to a hundred-foot oak tree. Unless you know trees, you'd have no idea of the potential of that little acorn. That's the difference between your current body and the one you will receive on that last day. "So is it with the resurrection of the dead. What is sown is perishable; what is raised is imperishable. It is sown in dishonor; it is raised in glory. It is sown in weakness; it is raised in power. It is sown a natural body; it is raised a spiritual body. If there is a natural body, there is also a spiritual body" (1 Corinthians 15:42–44).

I mentioned that my first wife died suddenly after her first chemo treatment. It wiped out her immune system, and she developed a colon infection. Before the doctors understood what was happening—all her systems were shutting down. In an effort to maintain her blood pressure, she was pumped full of fluids. She received thirty liters in two days, and she wasn't a big woman. It was gruesome. If I didn't know her specific room, my wife of twelve years would have been unrecognizable. The day she died I had a conversation in her hospital room with a couple friends about the resurrection body. The next day, I had the amazing realization that just as in her last days she was horrifically unrecognizable, so in her resurrected body she'll be gloriously restored, recognizable but—like the acorn which became the hundred-foot oak—transformed beyond our imaginations.

Eternal Pleasures

It is important to stress the continuity with our physical existence because it is so easy for us to slip into a Platonic vision of a spiritual eternity, like floating on clouds with harps. Many people rightly see this as a pretty boring existence. Why? Our most sublime pleasures touch both body and spirit. Consider listening to beautiful music that is both exquisite in composition and profoundly touches your heart. Think of the pleasure of a delicious meal with dear friends and delightful conversation. Then there's sexual expression that bonds body and soul. We are physical beings made for a physical eternity, and only that hope accurately anticipates the promise of eternal pleasure at his right hand (Psalm 16:11). As Paul contemplates the coming glory, he labels the pain of life in a fallen world and even the suffering that led him to despair of life as a "light momentary affliction" (2 Corinthians 4:17; also see 2 Corinthians 1:8). Paul understood that God has glorious things in store for those who believe his promises and trust that he "rewards those who seek him" (Hebrews 11:6).

Prior to serving at Harvest USA, I was involved in youth ministry. Teenagers think a lot about sex, so students would make comments such as, "Of course, I want Jesus to come back, but not before I get to have sex!" I suspect that many suffering with unsatisfied desires can relate to that sentiment, even if you'd never have the temerity to actually voice it. Since sex is one of the great pleasures of this world, it's understandable that no one would want to leave this life without experiencing it. But it shows how shortsighted we are and how limited our ability is to believe God's promises about eternal life in the new heavens and new earth. The first deception uttered in this world challenged the truthfulness and goodness of God (see Genesis 3:2). Whether we realize it or not, we all continue to wrestle with this lie. Like the father of the demon-possessed boy, I need to cry out, "I believe; help my unbelief" (Mark 9:24). That should be an ongoing prayer for all of us—that he'd give us grace to believe his promises in the midst of a fallen world. He has good in store and rewards those who seek him!

I think C. S. Lewis has the best response for those languishing without the experience of sexual pleasure in this life. He describes a situation in which a young boy first hears about the delights and pleasures of sex. His immediate response is to ask if you get to eat chocolates at the same time. It is the highest pleasure he knows. He can't imagine a pleasure that wouldn't include chocolate. Lewis says the boy could surmise the "absence of chocolates as the chief characteristic of sexuality. In vain would you tell him that the reason why lovers in their carnal raptures don't bother about chocolates is that they have something better to think of. The boy knows chocolate: he does not know the positive thing that excludes it." Lewis argues the same is true when people think of no sex in heaven as some kind of bland fast for eternity. He concludes, "We know the sexual life; we do not know, except in glimpses, the other thing which, in Heaven, will leave no room for it."[1] Lamenting the absence of sex in eternity is as laughable as a boy thinking he'll miss chocolate in the marriage bed. God has pleasures in store that you will need a resurrection body to even experience! The pleasures of the world to come wouldn't be endurable in our current fragile state. On the last day, when we enter the new heavens and new earth, no one is going to wish they had more sex. That idea will be ridiculous.

Living as God's Eschatological People

American Christians desperately need to rediscover our identity as God's eschatological people. What I mean is people who lose their life in this world because of the promise of eternal life, people who live as strangers and aliens because all their hope is placed in the world to come. This identity should inform all aspects of how we live our lives, especially our sexuality. Living with unsatisfied desires reminds us that this world is not our home. Scripture constantly points us beyond satisfaction in this life and urges us to stake all our hopes in Christ. I can live with unsatisfied desires now because the Day is coming when we'll know pleasure forevermore at his right hand. That's why unsatisfied desires are such a critical aspect of Christian discipleship. In some way, God asks all of us, "Will you wait on me? Will you trust me?"

This focus on our ultimate destiny motivates us to live differently in the here and now. John Lennon could not have been more wrong with his song "Imagine." There is a reason why the Bible ends with the book of Revelation. Living for the last day gives us the grace to live differently now. There is a hope and reason to live with reckless abandon for Christ and his kingdom—especially in relation to our material blessings—and to live soberly and reservedly regarding pleasure because he promises to satisfy the desires of our hearts. Church history records how early Christians turned pagan sensibilities on their head. In the Greco-Roman world, people were stingy with their money but generous with their bodies. There was a complete upheaval when they became Christians! Suddenly they became generous with their money and stingy with their bodies.

This is particularly true when we reflect on the call to deny ourselves and live for Christ. Especially for my single readers, it is a tall order to stake all your hopes on the kingdom of God. It is a source of utter bewilderment to the world. Consider Peter's assessment of the situation. Having described living for sex and partying, he concludes, "With respect to this they are surprised when you do not join them in the same flood of debauchery, and they malign you; but they will give account to him who is ready to judge the living and the dead" (1 Peter 4:4–5). Don't be shocked that you're misunderstood! When people turn away from life in God, sexual pleasure is often the greatest thing they know. They crave it more and more, even as the persistent itch begins to far outweigh any relief from the scratch. Peter doesn't negate the reality that self-denial and living by faith is hard. But did you catch Peter's conclusion? Pleasure will not have the last word. We'll give a full account of our lives before God. Self-denial matters because it is a tangible expression of faith in God's promises for the life to come in Christ.

The Waiting, Fasting King

Living without sex is really hard. During my darker moments as a single, I would occasionally say to God, "I hope it matters to you that I'm not masturbating!" (The Spirit's gentle response: "Yes, Dave. It matters.") In my more cynical moments, I'd think, "I know what's going to happen—I'll get remarried and then get prostate cancer!" Obviously, there were many areas of unbelief and struggles for me. The single life is not for the faint of heart! What I really needed was a clearer picture of Jesus.

Hebrews teaches that Jesus learned obedience through suffering and was made perfect by suffering (2:10; 5:8). We are told that "we do not have a high priest who is unable to sympathize with our weaknesses, but one who in every respect has been tempted as we are, yet without sin" (4:15). If we hold these two ideas together, we see that Jesus was tempted in every way that we are and (as 100 percent man) suffered in the midst of temptation but was victorious. That means he knows exactly the grace you need to endure temptation! Although many pagan religions have gods becoming men, usually to satisfy their own appetites, only Christianity has an incarnation that embraced suffering. A God who identifies with his people by suffering under the curse is the utterly unique center of the Christian faith. And this identification with us means he can be a real help. In fact, as Hebrews says elsewhere, "Because he himself has suffered when tempted, he is able to help those who are being tempted" (2:18). His personal suffering means that he is uniquely qualified to help you in your suffering.

And it goes even deeper. We are living in the age of the Spirit. What does this mean? When you are groaning under whatever current travail, Jesus is not far off in heaven, but right with you, empathetically recalling his own suffering. Jesus promised, "I will not leave you as orphans; I will come to you" (John 14:18). He also promised, "And behold, I am with you always, to the end of the age" (Matthew 28:20). The outpouring and filling of the Spirit means Jesus walks every step of this life with you. He has felt every sharp stone under your feet. He's endured every cutting word spoken to you. He has been wounded by every slight from others. All of us long to have someone who *really* gets it, who truly knows the depth of our experience and the challenges we face. Because Jesus's Spirit lives within us, he shares every trial you encounter and feels every moment of your groaning. He groans with us. This is why Paul describes the Spirit's intercession as "groanings too deep for words" (Romans 8:26). Not only is God not turned away from you in your frustrated desires, by his Spirit he personally enters into these very trials with you.

Further, Jesus is a waiting and fasting King. Contemplate this description of him: "he upholds the universe with the word of his power" (Hebrews 1:3). He is the ruling sovereign of the cosmos, but he still lives in humble submission. At one point as a single, I was studying the Gospels and a couple passages really jumped out at me. First, when Jesus talks about the timing of his return in glory on that last day, he said, "But concerning that day and hour no one knows, not even the angels of heaven, nor the Son, but the Father only" (Matthew 24:36). What does this mean? Jesus is still *waiting!* In his own experience, he continues to identify with us in our struggles. That didn't end with his ascension into heaven to rule. For two thousand years he's been waiting to return, perhaps patiently asking with each new morning, "Father, is it today?" He knows what it's like to endure for a *long time* with unsatisfied desires. Even in glory, he identifies with his people. And so he waits with us. As Hebrews promises, his suffering means he is able to be a help to you in your suffering. He knows the grace you need, and by his Spirit he will enable you to endure.

As we saw earlier, Jesus was eagerly looking forward to celebrating the Passover with his disciples. As he passed the cup at the Last Supper, he said,

> "Drink of it, all of you, for this is my blood of the covenant, which is poured out for many for the forgiveness of sins. I tell you I will not drink again of this fruit of the vine until that day when I drink it new with you in my Father's kingdom." (Matthew 26:27–29)

Jesus is choosing to deny himself this cup of celebration until we can all drink it together in the kingdom at the wedding feast. He left us instructions to feast all the time, remembering him and reminding ourselves of the coming consummation, but he is abstaining. He is choosing to fast from this cup of celebration until we can all sit down at the table together at the wedding feast of the marriage arranged by our Father before the foundation of the world.

The sacraments give us tangible reminders of our hope. My mother in-law's church has a little fountain just outside the door. In nice weather, they have baptisms in the courtyard. The idea is that each week as you are leaving you can dip your fingers into that gently bubbling water and *remember*. Similarly, with the Lord's Supper I always engage my five senses. I look at the bread and the cup. I purposely feel the bread with my fingers and roll the wine in my mouth. I smell the bread and the cup. I listen for the crunch of the bread as I eat, and I savor the taste. And I remind myself, Jesus's love for me is as real as these elements I am experiencing right now. He is present by his Spirit, just like these elements. Just as these elements are solid in the real world, so his promises to me are solid and trustworthy. It is impossible for him to lie. He knows our frames and weaknesses. He created us as physical beings and has left the sacraments as tangible reminders of the deep spiritual truths they signify and seal. We are set apart in baptism, and our transgressions are paid for in the body broken and nailed to the tree. The scarlet sins are washed whiter than snow by the blood poured out.

As you take those elements, hear his thrice-repeated promise in Revelation 22 to you, his bride:

"Behold, I am coming soon." (v. 7)

"Behold, I am coming soon, bringing my recompense with me, to repay each one for what he has done." (v. 12)

"Surely I am coming soon." (v. 20)

The day is rapidly approaching when the veil will be lifted. Pain and sorrow will flee away. And there will be One standing, whose beauty and majesty we can't fathom, with outstretched arms and nail-scarred hands. He will reach down, tenderly wiping the tears forever from our eyes, and give his invitation: "Arise, my love, my beautiful one, and come away, for behold, the winter is past; the rain is over and gone. The flowers appear on the earth, the time of singing has come, and the voice of the turtledove is heard in our land. The fig tree ripens its figs, and the vines are in blossom; they give forth fragrance. Arise, my love, my beautiful one, and come away" (Song of Solomon 2:10–13).

Acknowledgments

Tim Geiger and Scott Pickering, thank you for graciously approving an extended sabbatical so I could *finally* write this book.

Nicholas Black is an unflagging source of encouragement (even as he is also the Chief Grammar Nazi). Your reshaping of my wild and woolly first draft was invaluable to this finished product. And your constancy in friendship means so much to me.

To my generous supporters who have enabled me to serve at Harvest USA for over nineteen years, "I thank my God in all my remembrance of you . . . because of your partnership in the gospel from the first day until now" (Philippians 1:3, 5). I couldn't serve the King without you!

Thanks to the team at New Growth Press, especially Barbara Juliani and Ruth Castle, for your incredible patience after our initial conversation as the *years* of labor pains dragged on from idea to fruition.

David Smith, thank you, thank you, *thank you*. Now I understand when authors praise their editor for vastly improving the book. More importantly, you saved me (and everyone else!) from myself.

New Life Presbyterian Church of Glenside, thank you for providing my air-conditioned author's penthouse with a great view of the Easton Road corridor.

Jim Bergwall, I am deeply grateful for your faithful presence as spiritual director and prayer warrior. Mighty man of God, your wisdom is peppered throughout these pages.

Finally, Jennifer—a bright spring morning after bitter winter. My beautiful one, thank you for arising and coming away with me! This book would not exist apart from you. Our marriage provides ever-deepening awe of the "profound mystery." I love you.

Endnotes

Introduction

1. C. S. Lewis, *Mere Christianity* (New York: HarperOne, 1952), 48.

2. J. R. R. Tolkien, *The Return of the King* (New York: Ballantine Books, 1966), 246.

3. I realize this is an unusual experience and that many Christians intensely battle porn. If this is you, please take the time to go through these other New Growth Press resources: *Sexual Sanity for Men* (written by myself) or *Sexual Sanity for Women* (written by Harvest USA, edited by Ellen Dykas).

Chapter 1

1. "Six Reasons Young Christians Leave Church" Barna, 2011, accessed April 16, 2019, https://www.barna.com/research/six-reasons -young-christians-leave-church/.

2. Elizabeth Barrett Browning, "Aurora Leigh," in *The Complete Poetical Works of Mrs. Browning*, ed. Harriet Waters Preston (Boston: Houghton Mifflin, 1900), 372.

3. Other trinitarian references include Matthew 28:19; John 14:26; Acts 2:33; 2 Corinthians 13:14; Galatians 4:6; Ephesians 2:18; 1 Peter 1:2.

4. C. S. Lewis, *Mere Christianity*, 175.

5. Gordon J. Wenham, *Genesis 1–15, Volume 1,* Word Biblical Commentary (Grand Rapids: Zondervan, 1987), 68.

6. John Stott, *Our Social and Sexual Revolution: Major Issues for a New Century* (Grand Rapids: Baker Books, 1999), 199.

7. There is only one horrific experience of this union torn asunder, "My God, my God, why have you forsaken me?" (Matthew 27:46; Mark 15:34). And this was to secure their union with us for eternity!

8. See Todd Wilson, *Mere Sexuality: Rediscovering the Christian Vision of Sexuality* (Grand Rapids: Zondervan, 2017), 100.

9. Timothy Keller with Kathy Keller, *The Meaning of Marriage: Facing the Complexities of Commitment with the Wisdom of God* (New York: Penguin, 2011), 101.

Chapter 2

1. Kvetch is derived from the Yiddish *kvetchn*.

2. Following the death of Solomon, his son was trying to "be the man," oppressing and infuriating the people of Israel. This caused the rise of a rebel leader, Jeroboam, who ultimately led the northern ten tribes to secede from the nation of Israel, leaving only Judah and Benjamin to form the southern kingdom. Jeroboam made Samaria the capital of his kingdom. Ezekiel is written after Jerusalem was conquered by the Babylonians, and the prophet used this metaphor to demonstrate that Jerusalem's betrayal was worse than Samaria's.

3. Chronologically Hosea (eighth century BC) predates Jeremiah (seventh to fifth century BC) and Ezekiel (sixth century BC), but Hosea is located later in the biblical canon as the first Minor Prophet.

4. This deduction is supported by Derek Kidner, *The Message of Hosea: Love to the Loveless* (Downers Grove, IL: InterVarsity, 1981), 22.

Chapter 3

1. It is worth highlighting that Jesus anticipated that we'd be fasting right now as we await his return. There is something about deprivation that gets our attention. In our materialistic, decadent culture, most American Christians would benefit from rediscovering this largely lost spiritual discipline. I can say personally that fasting has been used by God to help sustain me spiritually during some very difficult seasons of my life. A helpful resource is John Piper, *A Hunger for God: Desiring God through Fasting and Prayer* (Wheaton, IL: Crossway, 1997).

2. See Westminster Confession of Faith 7.1, "The distance between God and the creature is so great, that although reasonable creatures do owe obedience unto him as their Creator, yet they could never have any fruition of him as their blessedness and reward, but by some voluntary condescension on God's part, which he hath been pleased to express by way of covenant."

3. For example, see Matthew Vines, *God and the Gay Christian: The Biblical Case in Support of Same-Sex Relationships* (New York: Convergent Books, 2014), 144–48.

4. Although I have experienced the truth of this, C. S. Lewis first pointed me to its reality. *The Four Loves* (New York: Harcourt, Brace and Company, 1960), 92.

5. This quote is shamelessly stolen from the title of Eugene Peterson's great book reflecting on the Psalms of Ascent. *A Long Obedience in the Same Direction: Discipleship in an Instant Society* (Downers Grove, IL: InterVarsity, 2000).

6. C. S. Lewis, *The Four Loves*, 176.

Chapter 4

1. C. S. Lewis, *Perelandra* (New York: Simon & Schuster, 1996), 42–43.

2. Saint Augustine, *Confessions*, trans. Henry Chadwick (New York: Oxford, 1991), 3.

3. John Freeman, *Hide or Seek: When Men Get Real with God about Sex* (Greensboro, NC: New Growth Press, 2014), 6.

4. F. F. Bruce, *1 and 2 Thessalonians, Volume 45*, Word Biblical Commentary (Grand Rapids: Zondervan, 1982), 83; Gordon D. Fee, *The First and Second Letters to the Thessalonians*, The New International Commentary on the New Testament (Grand Rapids: Eerdmans, 2009), 146.

5. For a helpful background to understand *The Song of Solomon*, see Tremper Longman III and Raymond B. Dillard, *An Introduction to the Old Testament*, 2nd ed. (Grand Rapids: Zondervan, 2006), 289–300.

6. Duane Garrett, *Song of Songs and Lamentations, Volume 23B*, Word Biblical Commentary (Grand Rapids: Zondervan, 2004), 223–24; Tremper Longman III, *Song of Songs*, The New International Commentary on the New Testament (Grand Rapids: Eerdmans, 2001), 173.

7. Marvin H. Pope, *Song of Songs*, The Anchor Bible Commentary (New York: Doubleday, 1977), 617; Longman, *Song*, 194–95; Iain M. Duguid, *Song of Songs*, Reformed Expository Commentary (Phillipsburg, NJ: P&R Publishing, 2016), 131–32.

8. I understand that if you are in a heterosexual marriage but struggling with same-sex attraction, or if for some other reason you're not physically attracted to your spouse, this can sound discouraging and make you feel even more "other." Remember, the invitation to relational oneness is the most fundamental characteristic of human sexuality. It is the emotional and spiritual union with another image-bearer that

makes for human sexuality! The physical attraction and being drawn to particular body parts is actually the most bestial aspect of our sexuality. It's what we share with the rest of the created order. My main point here is that the Bible says these things to indicate that God is utterly positive and celebratory of marital sexuality.

Chapter 5

1. D. A. Carson, *Matthew*, The Expositor's Bible Commentary (Grand Rapids: Zondervan, 1984), 178.

2. Wendell Berry, *Sex, Economy, Freedom, and Community* (New York: Pantheon Books, 1993), 134–35.

3. C. S. Lewis, *Mere Christianity*, 49.

4. William M. Struthers, *Wired for Intimacy: How Pornography Hijacks the Male Brain* (Downers Grove, IL: InterVarsity, 2009), 105–106.

Chapter 6

1. The acronym LGBTQ+ stands for Lesbian, Gay, Bisexual, Transgender, Queer (or Questioning). The "+" is today's attempt to be inclusive of the expression of further "sexual minorities." Other versions of the acronym also include I (Intersex) and A (Asexual).

2. Gareth Lee Cockerill, *The Epistle to the Hebrews*, The New International Commentary on the New Testament (Grand Rapids: Eerdmans, 2012), 682. The structure is a noun coupled with a predicate adjective.

3. Walter Bauer, et al., *A Greek-English Lexicon of the New Testament and Other Early Christian Literature* (University of Chicago Press, 2000), 693.

4. George Guthrie, *Hebrews*, The NIV Application Commentary (Grand Rapids: Zondervan, 1998), 683.

5. Craig Blomberg, *1 Corinthians*, The NIV Application Commentary (Grand Rapids: Zondervan, 1994), 132; F. F. Bruce, *1 and 2 Corinthians*, New Century Bible Commentary (London: Marshall, Morgan and Scott, 1971), 66.

6. Carolyn Mahaney in John Piper and Justin Taylor, eds., *Sex and the Supremacy of Christ* (Wheaton, IL: Crossway 2005), 201.

7. Peter Kreeft, "Is There Sex in Heaven?" accessed April 17, 2019, http://www.peterkreeft.com/topics/sex-in-heaven.htm.

Chapter 7

1. Kate Julian, "Why Are Young People Having So Little Sex?" *The Atlantic*, December 2019, https://www.theatlantic.com/magazine/

archive/2018/12/the-sex-recession/573949/. Warning: this article contains graphic language!

2. Tim Alan Gardner, *Sacred Sex: A Spiritual Celebration of Oneness in Marriage* (Colorado Springs: Waterbrook, 2002), 148–50.

3. For example, see Isaiah 11:6–9; 35:1–10; 65:17–15; Ezekiel 47:1–12; Revelation 21:1–22:5.

Chapter 8

1. Mel Gibson, Alan Ladd, Bruce Davey, Sophie Marceau, Patrick McGoohan, Catherine McCormack, James Horner, Steven Rosenblum, and Randall Wallace, *Braveheart* (Paramount, 2000).

2. The purity laws of the Old Testament excluded many from the tabernacle and temple, either for short periods of uncleanness or longer as in the case of eunuchs. But the point was not to reject certain people, rather the purity laws highlighted God's exalted holiness and distance from us. The great hope in the gospel is that the curtain was torn from top to bottom and Jesus opened the way for all of us to enter the holy place, right into God's presence with boldness (see Hebrews 4:16). Now there is no exclusion for any with infirmities or disabilities to draw near to God and fully engage in the community of God's people.

3. For a helpful discussion, see Todd Wilson, *Mere Sexuality*, 78–81.

4. A helpful resource for the church is Barry Danylak, *Redeeming Singleness: How the Storyline of Scripture Affirms the Single Life* (Wheaton, IL: Crossway, 2010).

5. Samuel Rutherford in Andrew A. Bonar, *Letters of Samuel Rutherford: With a Sketch of His Life and Biographical Notices of His Correspondents* (Edinburgh: Oliphant, Anderson, and Ferrier, 1984), 230.

6. "The Church's One Foundation," Samuel John Stone (1839–1900) / Music: Samuel Sebastian Wesley (1810–1876).

Chapter 9

1. "Everything Is Broken" is the title of a song from Bob Dylan's album *Oh Mercy* (Sony Music Entertainment, 1989).

2. Vines, *God and the Gay Christian*, 29.

3. Dale S. Kuehne, *Sex and the iWorld: Rethinking Relationships Beyond an Age of Individualism* (Grand Rapids: Baker Academic, 2009), 71.

4. Matthew Vines, "The Gay Debate: The Bible and Homosexuality," MatthewVines.com, accessed April 19, 2019.

5. C. S. Lewis, *Four Loves*, 87.

6. Lauren F. Winner, *Real Sex: The Naked Truth about Chastity* (Grand Rapids: Brazos, 2005), 50.

7. Bonnie Rochman, "Am I Pretty or Ugly? Why Teen Girls Are Asking YouTube for Validation," *Time*, March 7, 2012, http://healthland. time.com/2012/03/07/am-i-pretty-or-ugly-whats-behind-the-trend-of-girls-asking-youtube-for-validation/.

8. If this feels condemning, revisit the discussion on this passage in chapter 5, p. 79.

9. C. S. Lewis, *The Last Battle* (New York: Macmillan, 1956), 124.

10. Diane Mandt Langberg, *On the Threshold of Hope: Opening the Door to Healing for Survivors of Sexual Abuse* (Carol Stream, IL: Tyndale, 1999). Also see Justin and Lindsey Holcomb, *Is It My Fault? Hope and Healing for Those Suffering Domestic Violence* (Chicago: Moody, 2014).

11. Humanity's calling to rule over creation as God's stewards is central to Paul's argument for condemning both male and female homosexuality in Romans 1:18–27. Idolatry has fundamentally disordered the world, so humanity now worships in submission to that which we were created to rule. Homosexuality is an example of the disordering that occurs when humanity turns away from God and flips the created order upside down.

Chapter 10

1. Dan B. Allender and Tremper Longman III, *God Loves Sex: An Honest Conversation about Sexual Desire and Holiness* (Grand Rapids: Baker, 2014), 140.

2. As discussed in chapter 7, God's design establishes the framework whereby other behaviors, such as BDSM, are seen as clearly out of bounds, though not specifically addressed in the Bible.

3. Allender and Longman, *God Loves Sex*, 139–40.

4. See Gary Wilson, The Great Porn Experiment," TEDx Talk, May 16, 2012, https://www.youtube.com/watch?v=wSF82AwSDiU and other research articles on his website, including "Studies Linking Porn Use or Porn/Sex Addiction to Sexual Dysfunctions, Lower Arousal, and Lower Sexual and Relationship Satisfaction," Your Brain on Porn, accessed April 22, 2019, https://www.yourbrainonporn.com/relevant-research-and-articles-about-the-studies/porn-use-sex-addiction-studies/studies-linking-porn-use-or-porn-sex-addiction-to-sexual-dysfunctions-lower-arousal-and-lower-sexual-relationship-satisfaction/.

5. There are many helpful resources that engage the pro-gay theological interpretations of the prohibitive passages: R. Nicholas Black, *Homosexuality and the Bible: Outdated Advice or Words of Life?* (Greensboro, NC: New Growth Press, 2014); Kevin DeYoung, *What Does*

the Bible Really Teach about Homosexuality? (Wheaton, IL: Crossway, 2015); and Sam Allberry, *Is God Anti-Gay? And Other Questions about Homosexuality, the Bible and Same-Sex Attraction* (The Good Book Company, 2013). The most significant scholarly work on this topic is Robert A. J. Gagnon, *The Bible and Homosexual Practice: Texts and Hermeneutics* (Nashville: Abingdon, 2001).

6. For a fuller discussion on this topic, see my minibook, *Can You Change If You're Gay?* (Greensboro, NC: New Growth Press, 2013).

7. For example, see Jesse Singal, "When Children Say They're Trans," *The Atlantic*, July/August 2018, https://www.theatlantic.com/magazine/archive/2018/07/when-a-child-says-shes-trans/561749/.

Chapter 11

1. For a fuller discussion, see R. Nicholas Black, *iSnooping on Your Kids: Parenting in an Internet World* (Greensboro, NC: New Growth Press, 2012).

2. If you are unfamiliar with it, *Rent* is cast in the bohemian East Village of New York City and takes place over one year between New Year Eve celebrations in 1989 and 1990. The majority of the characters are HIV positive, and the fallout from their celebrated lifestyles is one of the deep, tragic ironies of the film. But the positive portrayals of the gay life, transgender, and free sex wildly contradict the scourge of AIDS resulting from the ideals celebrated by the musical.

3. Allender and Longman, *God Loves Sex*, 119–20.

4. If a wife is told by her husband to "submit" and not seek out pastoral help, counseling, and community, this is a gross distortion of biblical texts relating to marital dynamics. In such situations a wife should feel free to disregard the wishes of her husband. In a broken relationship, seeking help is wise, and refusing to do so is folly.

Chapter 12

1. See Rosaria Champagne Butterfield, *Secret Thoughts of an Unlikely Convert: An English Professor's Journey into Christian Faith* (Pittsburgh: Crown & Covenant, 2014), 1–27.

Chapter 13

1. C. S. Lewis, *Miracles: A Preliminary Study* (New York: HarperCollins, 1996), 261.

Harvest USA's mission is to bring the truth and mercy of Jesus Christ by:

- Helping individuals and families affected by sexual struggles
- Providing resources that address biblical sexuality to individuals and churches

We are a donor-supported ministry, so the churches and individuals who partner with us make it possible for us to produce resources like *God, You, & Sex: A Profound Mystery* and provide direct ministry to individuals and families, free of charge.

If you found this book helpful, consider partnering with us financially, advocating for our ministry in your local church, and/or praying for our work.

For free resources, please visit harvestusa.org.

Harvest USA
715 Twining Road, Suite 200
Dresher, PA 19025
215-482-0111
info@harvestusa.org

Also Available from Harvest USA and New Growth Press